STRENGTH TRAINING

Beginners, Bodybuilders, Athletes

Third Edition

Philip E. Allsen
Brigham Young University

KENDALL/HUNT PUBLISHING COMPANY
4050 Westmark Drive   Dubuque, Iowa 52002

Chairman and Chief Executive Officer   Mark C. Falb
Vice President, Director of National Book Program   Alfred C. Grisanti
Editorial Development Manager   Georgia Botsford
Developmental Editor   Tina Bower
Prepress Project Coordinator   Sheri Hosek
Prepress Editor   Lynne Rogers
Permissions Editor   Renae Heacock
Design Manager   Jodi Splinter
Designer   Suzanne Millius
Senior Vice President, College Division   Thomas W. Gantz
Vice President and National Field Manager   Brian Johnson
Managing Editor, College Field   John Coniglio
Associate Editor, College Field   Charles Ward

Printed in the United States of America
10 9 8 7 6 5 4 3 2 1

About the Author

Philip E. Allsen is professor of physical education and director of the Fitness for Life program at Brigham Young University in Provo, Utah. Widely known for his expertise in physical fitness, sports medicine, and athletic conditioning, Dr. Allsen has written sixteen books and authored more than one hundred articles on the topics of strength and physical fitness. The Fitness for Life program, which he developed at Brigham Young University, now serves approximately seven thousand students at the institution each year and has been adopted by more than four hundred schools in the United States.

Dr. Allsen has served as a conditioning consultant to a large number of professional athletes and professional teams. He is a member of the American College of Sports Medicine; the American Alliance of Health, Physical Education, Recreation and Dance; the National Collegiate Physical Education Association; and the National Strength and Conditioning Association.

PREFACE

Anyone who is interested in increasing their performance, whether in athletics or any other aspect of life, can do so by increasing body strength. *Strength Training: Beginners, Bodybuilders, Athletes* presents strength development programs for beginning strength trainers, for those who wish to improve their athletic ability, and for those interested in becoming serious bodybuilders.

I have had the opportunity to supervise strength training programs for thousands of people, ranging from individuals who have never participated in any type of strength program to elite athletes who compete on a professional level. Physique athletes who have been strength trained have gone on to win national contests in bodybuilding.

The first two chapters of this book give the scientific background on the physiological and anatomical changes brought about by engaging in a strength development program. The basic concepts necessary to understand strength programs are also presented in these two chapters.

The remaining chapters deal with the actual design of specific strength training programs. These chapters present many different exercises for each of the particular muscle groups to help readers develop a total and comprehensive training program. Readers may select from among a variety of exercises to strengthen the various body parts. Each exercise is illustrated by pictures that demonstrate correct body position and technique. The pictures are accompanied by explanations of the action, as well as precautions to take. Readers who apply these concepts can easily design programs that are safe and efficient.

Strength training is important for everyone. This type of training can ensure greater productivity in many areas of life, as well as enable practitioners to enjoy the positive benefits of an enhanced self-concept.

CONTENTS

Why Train for Strength?

CHAPTER 1

Often when the word *strength* enters into a conversation, people think of men with bulging muscles or NFL football players crashing into one another on the field of battle. People then ask why ordinary individuals should give serious consideration to engaging in a strength training program. Sometimes people make statements such as, "What good will increased strength do for me in my business as a computer programmer?"

To answer these questions and dispel some of the misconceptions surrounding the topic of strength, let us consider what strength is and why strength can give everyone an advantage in participating in the activities of daily life.

STRENGTH AND ITS ADVANTAGES

Strength is defined as the ability to exert force against resistance. Force is the basis of all motion, and when we examine the world we live in, we can easily observe that it is a world of motion. Strength then becomes an important aspect in performing the tasks of daily living, such as lifting, walking, running, doing housework, and engaging in recreational tasks.

Another aspect of movement is *power.* Power is defined as the rate at which energy can be released, or the rate of doing work. The formula for power is as follows:

$$\text{Power} = \text{Force} \times \frac{\text{Displacement in the direction of force}}{\text{Time}}$$

Displacement in the direction of force divided by time equals velocity. Thus, the two factors that influence power are force (strength) and velocity. To affect power, a training program must affect either strength or velocity or, if possible, both of these factors at the same time. Of these two variables, it is much more difficult to bring about changes in velocity than in strength. Thus, the key to developing increased power is the change that a training program can bring about on the development of strength.

In this way, power becomes one of the keys to a more productive life. It is not time itself that is important but rather what takes place in that time; productivity determines the difference between success and failure. By increasing your power output, you can accomplish more work in a shorter period of time.

Consider the practical example of mowing the lawn. If you increase your strength and bring about a greater power output, the work of mowing the lawn can be accomplished much more quickly. A friend gave the following reason for participating in a strength program: "I can finish my yard work in a short period of time, and this allows me to get on the golf course where I can apply force to the golf ball with a great amount of joy!"

The past few years have seen some remarkable performances in athletic achievement. Athletes are jumping farther and higher, runners are breaking records in most of the running events, and swimming records are broken in nearly every large swimming meet.

Physiologically, the body has been operating the same way for a long while, so there must be a reason why the human body is breaking athletic records that were thought to be impossible to change. When we examine the training procedures these record-breaking athletes engage in, we find that one of the greatest causes of improvement is the proper use of a strength training program.

If strength is the ability to exert force and force is a tendency to cause motion, then strength is important not only to the athlete but also to all individuals in everyday life. If more work can be accomplished in a shorter period of time, a person is more powerful. If all else remains equal, an increase in strength will contribute to an improvement in the performance of the human body.

Another reason for engaging in strength training is that it makes you feel better and look better. A person does not have to be a so-called bodybuilder to value how an attractive body can have a positive effect on self-concept. In a survey of the men and women engaged in a series of strength development classes, over 80 percent responded that the major reason for taking the class was that they wished "to look better."

Since many people express a desire to look better, a discussion of body composition is important. The human body is composed of materials that are referred to as *lean body mass* and *fat mass*. Lean body mass is made up primarily of muscle tissue, connective tissue, bone, and fluids, and fat mass is the fat that the body stores. Many people in our society have an excess amount of body fat, and this leads to the problem of obesity. One estimate is that by the age of fifty, almost 50 percent of the people in the United States are approaching obesity, or overfatness.

The relationship between the amount of muscle mass in the body and excess body fat is often overlooked. The amount and size of muscle decrease in many people as they get older because of a lack of a strength training stimulus. As muscle mass decreases, the person uses less energy even at rest, and a greater percentage of the body weight becomes fat. Fat tissue does not burn nearly as many calories at rest as muscle tissue, and thus the individual continues to gain body fat. In other words, many people become fat because they are using fewer calories as a result of the loss of muscle mass caused by a lack of activity. Since people spend more time in sitting than in any other activity, the average American becomes overfat as he or she grows older.

Ancel Keys, a researcher in weight control, showed that the decrease in caloric expenditure in different age groups at rest was related to the change in muscle mass rather than to age. For example, at age sixty a person will use approximately fifteen calories less per hour than a person who is twenty-six years of age. Over a twenty-four-hour period this would be a total of 360 unused calories per day. If that person wanted to retain the same eating habits but not put on fat, he or she would have to walk approximately six miles each day to expend the 360 calories, since the energy used in walking one mile is about sixty calories. The sixty-year-old individual, therefore, must increase activity, decrease caloric intake, or else put on more fat.

A person can help eliminate the problem of overfatness by using a strength development program to maintain muscle mass so that caloric expenditure at rest won't decrease. Thus a person won't have to exercise so extensively to combat obesity. The body will continue to use more calories if muscle mass is maintained throughout life.

A common misconception about strength development is that a strength training program will cause "muscle-boundness," or a loss of flexibility. Many scientific studies indicate that the opposite is true—that engaging in a strength program correctly will actually bring about an improvement in flexibility. One study, conducted at the 1972 Olympic Games, tested the flexibility of the competing athletes and found that the most flexible athletes were the gymnasts, swimmers, and weightlifters.

The key to maintaining good flexibility is to take the body parts through a full range of motion. This can be accomplished by engaging in a proper strength development program. By using correct techniques, you will develop strength throughout the entire range of movement of the body musculature.

The ability of the body to resist the stresses that can result from an injury can be increased by obtaining a greater amount of strength. In the athletic world, statistics indicate that athletic injuries, such as in football, are reduced when teams engage in a strength development program. The fatigue of sports participation combats the body's ability to withstand the disruption of movement, but with an increase in strength, the athlete is more powerful and thus retains the ability to perform in the later stages of the contest. This same advantage is important in performing everyday tasks, such as lifting or carrying objects.

HEALTH BENEFITS OF STRENGTH TRAINING

Besides increasing strength, creating more collagenous fibrils in connective tissue, bringing about changes in nervous tissue, and increasing bone density, a strength training program has other health benefits.

Some of the risk factors for coronary heart disease (CHD) are determined by the variables of blood cholesterol and blood lipids and the transport molecules known as lipid proteins. A total body strength program has a positive effect on these variables.

High blood sugar (glucose) levels and high insulin levels are risk factors for diabetes and CHD. Recent evidence has revealed that strength training can bring about positive changes in glucose metabolism.

Colon cancer is associated with a prolonged gastrointestinal transit time, and sedentary living is associated with an increase of cancer of the colon. An accelerated transit time is associated with a strength training program that develops the abdominal musculature. One study found that strength training brought about an average acceleration of 56 percent in gastrointestinal transit time after thirteen weeks of training.

WOMEN AND STRENGTH TRAINING

Women considering strength training are sometimes concerned that strength exercises will make them appear less feminine. The fear is that training will produce large, unsightly, bulging muscles. In the past few years, research has disputed this myth. Women have the same muscle properties as men, but because of endocrinological differences, they respond to a training stimulus in different ways. Before puberty, there is little difference between the muscular size and strength of boys and girls, but with the onset of puberty, testosterone from the testes of the male and estrogen from the ovaries of the female begin to enter the bloodstream and trigger the development of the appropriate secondary sexual characteristics. The result is that men develop a greater quantity of muscle tissue and respond with a greater gain of muscle mass when they engage in a strength program.

In most cases, women will not gain a large amount of muscle mass when training, but they will obtain increased strength, which will enable them to better perform daily activities. The diameter of a muscle cell can increase as much as 30 percent without measurable growth in the girth of a body limb, so women do not have to worry about increased body size. There is no physiological reason for women not to engage in a strength training program and no need to suggest different training programs on the basis of sex. Both women and men can experience the same general benefits; it is only the degree of gain in muscle tissue that will differ.

STRENGTH TRAINING FOR THOSE OVER FORTY

Some people ask whether those over the age of forty should engage in strength training. The answer is that all the advantages of increased strength hold true for any age.

Research comparing the rate of strength gains in men and women of various ages shows that the rates are similar for all age groups. One study used men and women with an average age of ninety. After strength training for eight weeks in a three-day-per-week program, the subjects experienced a 174 percent increase in strength.

Our youth-oriented society tends to neglect the needs of its older citizens. If you are an individual who falls into the over-forty category, rest assured that engaging in a proper strength development program can not only increase your strength but also increase the overall performance of your body.

STRENGTH TRAINING AND CHILDREN

Another question involves whether strength training is an appropriate activity for children before the age of pubescence. At one time the assumption was that prepubescent boys and girls could not increase strength because of a lack of adult hormones. A large amount of research indicates that this assumption is false and that children can obtain significant strength gains in a properly designed program.

Other research has revealed that a strength training program will also contribute to motor performance gains and other health-related benefits such as injury prevention, improvements in blood lipid profiles, an increase in bone density, and a positive effect on body composition. Strength training also has been found to contribute to a more positive self-concept and body image in children.

The National Strength and Conditioning Association and the American Orthopaedic Society for Sports Medicine have stated that proper strength training will have lasting benefits on young participants. They have suggested the following guidelines in the design of strength programs for this age group:

1. Require a medical examination before participating in the strength program.
2. Make sure the training facility provides a safe exercise environment.
3. Participants should have the emotional maturity to accept and follow proper training directions.
4. Instructors should be qualified and remember the uniqueness of each child.
5. Include warm-up and cool-down exercises in the training program.
6. Demonstrate proper exercise techniques for each exercise utilized in the program.
7. Increase the resistance gradually as strength improves in the participants.

8. Prohibit one repetition maximum lifts during the program to prevent possible injury.
9. Remember that strength training is part of an overall conditioning program.

These guidelines are excellent suggestions not only for children but also for any strength trainer regardless of age.

CONCLUSION

An examination of all the ways strength can contribute to the overall efficiency of the human body reveals that a strength development program should be a lifetime process. When you make the decision to start a strength program, you have started a new lifestyle. Maintaining that lifestyle is important, since strength is reversible and will decline if you do not continue to obtain a strength stimulus for your entire life.

Principles and Programs

CHAPTER **2**

MOTOR UNITS

The human body has about 434 muscle groups that are used to move the various parts of the anatomy. Each one of these muscles is made up of what are known as *motor units*. A motor unit is composed of a single motor neuron and all of the muscle cells innervated by this neuron. Figure 2.1 is a diagram of motor units.

All motor units do not have the same capabilities and are classified as either slow-twitch, fast-twitch a, or fast-twitch b motor units. Table 2.1 summarizes the characteristics of the various motor units. An individual muscle is composed of both fast-twitch and slow-twitch muscle cells. Fast-twitch cells have the ability to contract very rapidly and thus generate a large amount of force in a short period of time. They expend their energy sources quickly and thus are more easily fatigued.

Slow-twitch cells can exert force for longer periods of time and are used for activities that require submaximum force, such as jogging, walking, and long-distance swimming. Even though genetics determines whether we have muscles composed of a greater percentage of slow-twitch cells or fast-twitch cells, strength training can affect the ability of both cells to exert force.

During the contraction of a muscle, motor unit recruitment is greatly affected by the force necessary to perform the movement. Slow-twitch motor units are usually recruited to lift a light weight. However, in lifting a heavy weight, all of the motor units might have to be recruited. *Ramp effect* refers to the relationship between the percentage of muscle fibers used

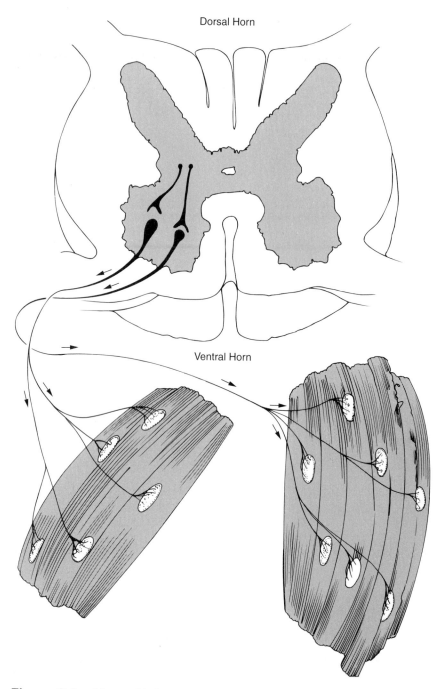

Dorsal Horn

Ventral Horn

Figure 2.1 Motor Units

Table 2.1 Characteristics of Fast-Twitch (FT$_a$, FT$_b$) and Slow-Twitch (ST) Motor Units

Characteristic	ST	FT$_a$	FT$_b$
NEURAL ASPECTS			
Motoneuron size	Small	Large	Large
Motoneuron recruitment threshold	Low	High	High
Motor nerve conduction velocity	Slow	Fast	Fast
STRUCTURAL ASPECTS			
Muscle fiber diameter	Small	Large	Large
Mitochondrial density (aerobic energy)	High	High	Low
Capillary density	High	Medium	Low
Myoglobin (aerobic) density	High	Medium	Low
ENERGY SUBSTRATE			
Creatine phosphate stores	Low	High	High
Glycogen (carbohydrate) stores	Low	High	High
Triglyceride (fat) stores	High	Medium	Low
ENZYMATIC ASPECTS			
Glycolytic (anaerobic) enzyme activity	Low	High	High
Oxidative (aerobic) enzyme activity	High	High	Low
FUNCTIONAL ASPECTS			
Twitch (contraction) time	Slow	Fast	Fast
Relaxation time	Slow	Fast	Fast
Force production	Low	High	High
Fatigue resistance	High	Low	Low
DISTRIBUTION			
Endurance athletes	High	Medium to high	Low
Sprint, explosive athletes	Medium to low	Medium to high	High

and the amount of muscular force required to recruit motor units. Figure 2.2 illustrates this idea.

One important implication of the ramp effect is how it may affect a strength training program. To increase the potential of all of the motor units, especially the potential of the fast-twitch motor units, the training must be of a fairly high intensity. The use of a proper strength program allows all of the motor units to be stimulated and thus increases their capability to become stronger and exert a greater force.

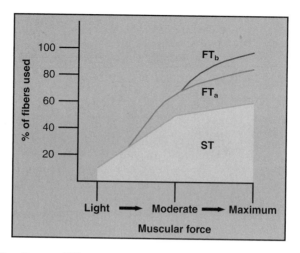

Figure 2.2   Ramp Effect

Motor unit type is usually determined in the laboratory by an invasive procedure that involves collecting a small sample of muscle tissue using a needle biopsy. The muscle sample is then chemically analyzed to determine the ratio of various motor units contained in the muscle.

A field test can be used to obtain a rough estimation of motor unit type within a muscle group. The following procedures are used to estimate motor unit type:

1. Establish a one-repetition maximum (1 RM) for the specific lift.
2. Perform as many repetitions as possible using 80 percent of the 1 RM.
   a. If you can complete only a few repetitions (less than seven), then the muscle group is likely composed of more than 50 percent fast-twitch motor units.
   b. If you can complete many repetitions (more than twelve), then the muscle group likely has more than 50 percent slow-twitch motor units.
   c. If you can only complete between seven and twelve repetitions, then the muscle group probably has an equal proportion of slow-twitch and fast-twitch muscle units.

JOINT-LEVER SYSTEM

Many times when people think of a strength training program, they only consider changes that take place in the muscle tissue. Movement in the

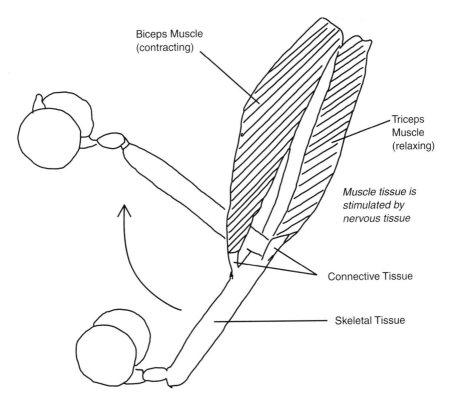

Figure 2.3 Joint-Lever System

body is produced through the use of joint-lever systems, which are composed of nervous tissue, connective tissue, skeletal tissue, and muscle tissue. A proper strength training program may increase the output of a joint-lever system by bringing about changes in one or more of the various tissues. Figure 2.3 is an example of a joint-lever system.

The exact physiological cause of increased strength is not known, but an examination of research reveals that changes that take place in the joint-lever system might contribute to an increase in strength. An indication of these sites is contained in figure 2.4.

Nervous Tissue: As a result of a strength program, a neural adaptation could bring about an increased neural drive to muscle. This has been indicated by the use of electromyographic (EMG) studies. Other changes in the nervous system may bring about a possible increased synchronization of the motor units that make up the various muscle groups, and this might contribute to increased strength.

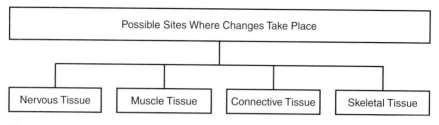

Figure 2.4 Changes in the Joint-Lever System

Sensory units located in the tendons, known as Golgi tendon organs, when stimulated by tension placed on a joint-lever system, cause a muscle to relax. A strength program may bring about changes that partly inhibit this mechanism and allow a greater force to be produced by the muscle. Much of the increased strength output in the first few weeks of a strength training program is thought to be due to changes in the nervous system.

Connective Tissue: The body uses connective tissue to hold bones and muscles together. Connective tissue is also used to transmit the force of a muscle contraction to the bone or lever arm of the joint-lever system. Very few muscles are directly attached to the bone by muscle alone. The muscle is usually attached to a tendon, which is composed of connective tissue. To transmit the force, the connective tissue relies on many collagenous fibrils, which are primarily composed of protein. Figure 2.5 is a diagram of connective tissue. A proper strength training program increases these fibrils and thus increases the capability of connective tissue to transmit force to the bone.

Skeletal Tissue: Skeletal tissue is used to construct the levers in a joint-lever system. A proper strength training program increases the deposit of mineral salts in the skeletal tissue and thus increases bone density.

Osteoporosis is a condition of increased porosity and decreased bone mineral density. More women die each year from problems resulting from hip fractures related to osteoporosis than from the combination of deaths from breast cancer, uterine cancer, and ovarian cancer. Osteoporosis might be prevented if the prevention starts early enough in a person's life. Two major factors that can help to prevent osteoporosis are weight-bearing exercises and a proper diet with adequate calcium. Adolescent boys and girls should have a daily intake of at least 1,200 milligrams of calcium, and adults should take in at least 1,000 milligrams per day. After

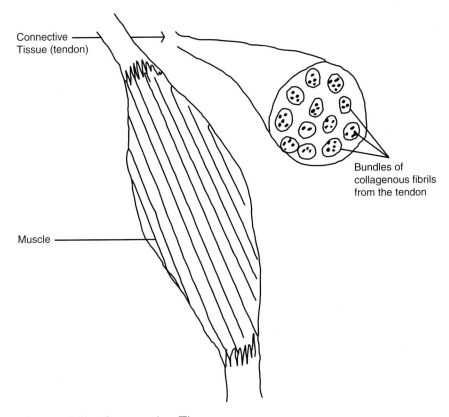

Connective
Tissue (tendon)

Bundles of
collagenous fibrils
from the tendon

Muscle

Figure 2.5 Connective Tissue

menopause, women should have a daily intake of at least 1,500 milligrams per day.

Regular weight-bearing exercise will help prevent osteoporosis. Increasing the amount of resistance, such as in strength training, may provide the body with an effective stimulus to cause an increase in the density of the bone. Research reveals that the forces produced on certain bones, such as the lumbar vertebrae in the back, during walking and jogging are 1.75 times the body's weight. During a strength training program using weights, the loads may be as much as 5 to 6 times the body's weight. Thus, the results of a strength training program have beneficial effects on skeletal tissue.

Muscle Tissue: Because of its ability to contract, muscle tissue is the only tissue in the body that has the capability to produce a force. Figure 2.6 contains a diagram of the components of a muscle cell.

A muscle is made up of many muscle cells known as motor units. To increase the strength of the muscle, usually an increase in the size of the muscle must occur. *Hypertrophy, hyperplasia,* and *atrophy* are terms that are useful in understanding how a muscle might become larger or smaller:

Hypertrophy: Increase in cell size

Hyperplasia: Increase in number of cells

Atrophy: Decrease in cell size and/or a decrease in cell number

Research indicates that the major change in muscle tissue as a result of a strength training program is due to hypertrophy of the muscle cells.

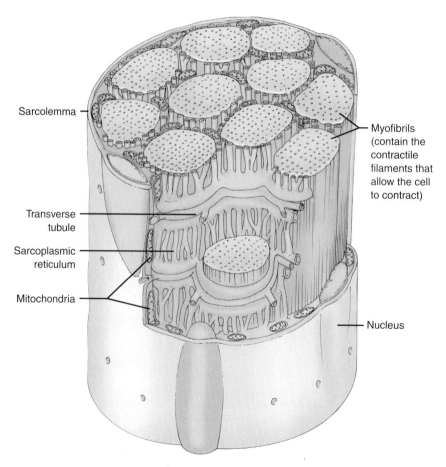

Figure 2.6 Muscle Cell

An examination of figure 2.6 reveals that a muscle cell is made up of bundles called myofibrils. Myofibrils contain the contractile filaments that allow the muscle cell to contract. The stimulus of a strength training program appears to release chemical modulators that cause the myofibrils to split and activate chemical mechanisms that increase the amount of contractile filaments within the myofibrils. This increased mass allows the cell to exert a greater force and become stronger.

Muscles can also become weaker through the process of atrophy, which is a decrease in the size of a cell due to loss of myofibrils and contractile filaments. Atrophy also refers to a loss of muscle cells. As explained earlier, a muscle is composed of motor units that are classified as slow-twitch, fast-twitch a, and fast-twitch b motor units. To stimulate or overload the fast-twitch motor units, you must utilize relatively high resistance. If these motor units are not used, they begin to atrophy. The fast-twitch motor units are highly susceptible to atrophy, especially after the age of twenty-five. Once these cells are lost, the body cannot restore them. This is one of the reasons why strength training should be a lifelong activity.

WEAKEST JOINT ANGLE PRINCIPLE

As a joint-lever system goes through a full range of motion, the ability to exert force at different joint angles changes. Figure 2.7 illustrates this concept.

A muscle exerts the greatest force when it is in a slightly stretched position. Another factor that affects the production of force is the mechanical alignment of the bones that make up the lever arms. This factor is referred to as *mechanical advantage,* or the ratio of the force arm to the resistance arm. For example, the most advantageous joint angle during arm flexion, using the biceps, is thought to be approximately when the elbow is flexed at a 100° angle. Thus when a joint-lever system is working through a range of motion, the variables of muscle length and mechanical advantage are going to have an effect on the force produced by the system.

Some machines supposedly have the capability to apply maximum resistance at every joint angle through a range of motion. This might appear to be an advantage, as shown in figure 2.8. These machines are known as *accommodating resistance machines* and are based on the principle of using either isokinetic or variable resistance. In real-life move-

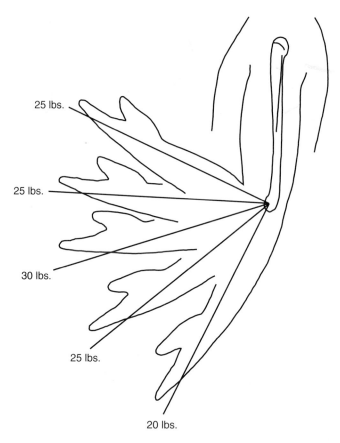

25 lbs.

25 lbs.

30 lbs.

25 lbs.

20 lbs.

Figure 2.7 Change of Ability to Exert Force Through a Range of Motion

ments, however, using the joint-lever systems of the body through a full range of motion, the system will always be limited by the weakest joint angle.

MAJOR HUMAN MUSCLES

Familiarity with basic anatomy and various movements of the human body is necessary in designing weight training programs. Figure 2.9 contains a diagram of the major human muscles, and table 2.2 lists the name of the muscle, the action of the muscle, and the sport in which the muscle is used. By using this information, you can analyze a sport to determine the most important movements and the muscles involved. For example,

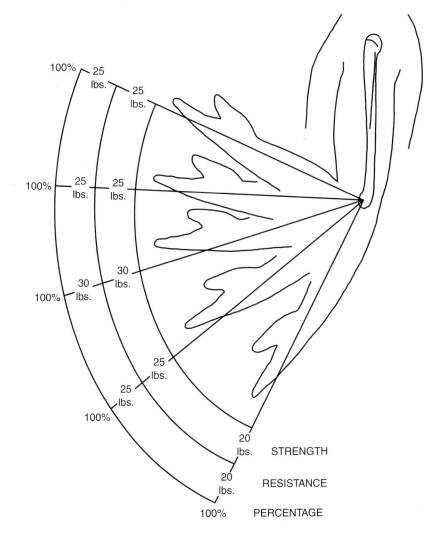

Figure 2.8 Accommodating Resistance Concept

muscle no. 26, the trapezius, tilts the head back, elevates the shoulder point, and adducts the scapula. This muscle is used in the wrestler's bridge, passing a football, and cleaning a barbell, as well as in the breast-stroke, archery, and batting.

Regardless of the training method chosen, the overload principle, discussed next, must be utilized to obtain strength gains, and the resistance must be progressively increased as the muscles increase in strength.

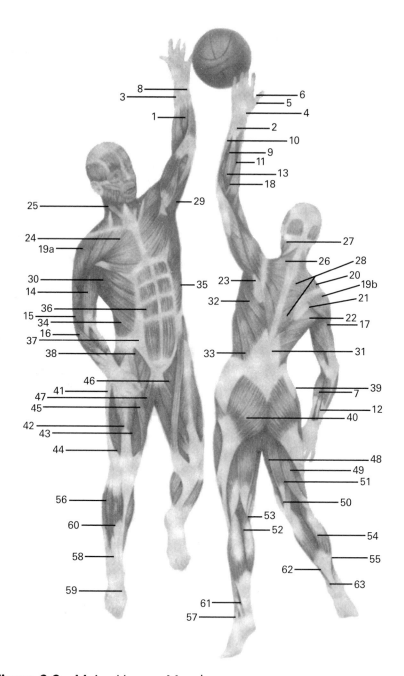

Figure 2.9 Major Human Muscles

Table 2.2 Muscle Action and Sport Use

Supinate: rotate forearm to palms-up
Invert: turn sole of foot inward
Evert: turn sole of foot outward
Elevate: raise a part against gravity
Depress: lower a part, yielding to gravity
Lateral: located toward the outer side
Medial: located toward the middle
Flex: bend at a joint, decreasing angle

Extend: straighten at a joint
Adduct: move toward midline of body
Abduct: move away from midline
Rotate: move part around an axis
Prone: face downward
Supine: face upward
Pronate: rotate forearm to palms-down

Muscle	Primary Action (numbers in parentheses indicate muscles that assist)	Sport in Which Greatest Resistance is Encountered
1. Flexor digitorum-profundus	Flexes fingers	Any sport in which one grasps an opponent, partner, or equipment, such as wrestling, hand-to-hand balancing, tennis, horizontal bar, ball bat, etc.
2. Extensor digitorum	Extends fingers	
3. Flexor pollicis longus	Flexes thumb	
4. Extensor pollicis longus	Extends thumb	
5. Abductor pollicis longus	Abducts thumb	
6. Adductor pollicis longus	Adducts and flexes thumb	
7. Flexor carpi radialis	Flexes wrist palmward (8), abducts hand (9)	Tennis, throwing a baseball, passing a football, handball, ring work, two-handed pass in basketball, batting, golf swing
8. Flexor carpi ulnaris	Flexes wrist palmward (7), adducts hand (10)	
9. Extensor carpi radialis longus and brevis	Extends wrist (10), abducts hand (7)	Backhand stroke in tennis and badminton, Olympic weight lifting, bait and fly casting
10. Extensor carpi ulnaris	Extends wrist (9), adducts hand (8)	

Continued.

Muscle	Primary Action (numbers in parentheses indicate muscles that assist)	Sport in Which Greatest Resistance is Encountered
11. Pronator teres 12. Pronator quadratus	Pronates forearm	Tennis forehand, shot put, throwing a punch, throwing a baseball, passing a football
13. Supinator	Supinates forearm (16)	Throwing a curve ball, batting, fencing thrust
14. Biceps brachii 15. Brachialis	Flexes forearm (16)	Ring work, rope climb, archery, pole vaulting, wrestling, backstroke in swimming
16. Brachioradialis	Flexes forearm, supinates forearm	Rowing, cleaning a barbell, rope climb
17. Triceps brachii 18. Anconeus	Extends forearm	Breaststroke, shot put, parallel bar work, vaulting, hand shivers in football, hand balancing, batting pole vaulting, fencing thrust, passing, boxing
19. Deltoid 　　Anterior fibers 　　Posterior fibers 20. Supraspinatus 21. Infraspinatus 22. Teres minor	Abducts humerus (20) Flexes humerus Extends humerus Abducts humerus (19) Rotates humerus laterally	Hand balancing, canoeing, shot put, pole vaulting, tennis, archery, batting, fencing thrust, passing a football, tackling, breaststroke, back and crawl strokes, golf swing, handball

Muscle	Primary Action (numbers in parentheses indicate muscles that assist)	Sport in Which Greatest Resistance is Encountered
23. Teres major	Adducts, extends, and rotates humerus medially (32)	Rope climb, canoe racing, ring work, rowing, batting, crawl, back, breast, and butterfly strokes, pole vaulting, golf
24. Pectoralis major	Adducts, flexes, and rotates humerus	Tackling, crawl, and backstrokes, tennis, passing a football, throwing a baseball, javelin, pole vaulting, wrestling, shot put, discus throw, straight-arm lever position in gymnastics, punching
25. Sternocleidomastoid	Flexes and laterally flexes neck, rotates head (27)	Crawl stroke, tucking chin in wrestling, football, boxing, distance running (breathing)
26. Trapezius	Bends head laterally toward shoulder	Wrestler's bridge
	Elevates shoulder	Passing a football, cleaning a barbell, breaststroke
	Adducts scapula	Archery, batting, breaststroke
27. Splenius cervicis/ capitus	Extends head back Extends head (26) Rotates head	
28. Major and minor rhomboids, levator scapulae	Adducts and rotates scapula medially, depresses shoulder	Tennis backhand, batting, back and breaststroke

Continued.

Muscle	Primary Action (numbers in parentheses indicate muscles that assist)	Sport in Which Greatest Resistance is Encountered
29. Subscapularis	Rotates humerus medially (24), stabilizes humerus in glenoid cavity to prevent displacement	Tackling, crawl and backstrokes, tennis, passing a football, throwing a baseball, javelin, pole vaulting, wrestling, shot put, discus throw, straight-arm level position in gymnastics
30. Serratus anterior	Abducts scapula	Shot put, discus throw, tennis, archery, tackling, crawl stroke, passing a basketball, passing a football, punching
31. Erector spinae	Extends vertebral column	Discus and hammer throw, batting, golf swing, racing start in swimming, diving and tumbling, rowing, blocking in football
32. Latissimus dorsi	Adducts, extends, and rotates humerus medially; depresses shoulder	Rope climb, canoe racing, ring work, rowing, batting, crawl, back, breast, and butterfly strokes, pole vaulting, golf swing
33. Quadratus lumborum	Flexes vertebral column, flexes vertebral column laterally	The importance of this group in all sports, posture, and general fitness and appearance cannot be overstated

Muscle	Primary Action (numbers in parentheses indicate muscles that assist)	Sport in Which Greatest Resistance is Encountered
34. External abdominal oblique	Flexes and rotates vertebral column	The importance of this group in all sports, posture, and general fitness and appearance cannot be overstated
35. Internal abdominal oblique		
36. Rectus abdominus	Flexes vertebral column (33)	
37. Transverse abdominus	Compresses abdomen	
38. Iliopsoas, pectineus	Flexes femur (42)	Running, hurdling, pole vaulting, kicking a football, line play, flutter kick, pike and tuck positions in diving and tumbling
39. Gluteus medius	Abducts femur, rotates femur medially	Hurdling, fencing, frog kick, shot put, running, line play, skating
40. Gluteus maximus	Extends femur, rotates femur laterally	Skiing, shot put, running, quick starts in track, all jumping and skipping, line play, skating, swimming start, changing directions while running
41. Tensor fasciae	Flexes, abducts, and rotates femur medially	

Continued.

Muscle	Primary Action (numbers in parentheses indicate muscles that assist)	Sport in Which Greatest Resistance is Encountered
42. Rectus femoris	Extends lower leg (43, 44), flexes femur	Skiing, skating, quick starts, all jumping, kick in football or soccer, flutter kick, frog kick, water skiing, diving, trampoline and tumbling, bicycling, catching in baseball
43. Vastus medialis	Extends lower leg	
44. Vastus lateralis		
45. Sartorius	Flexes lower leg, flexes femur, rotates femur laterally	
46. Adductor magnus	Adducts femur (48)	Skiing, skating, frog kick, broken field running, bareback horseback riding
47. Adductor longus		
48. Gracilis	Adducts femur, flexes lower leg	
49. Biceps femoris	Flexes lower leg, rotates lower leg laterally (53, 54); extends femur (48, 50, 51)	Skiing, skating, quick starts in track and swimming, hurdling line play, all jumping
50. Semimembranosus	Flexes lower leg, rotates lower leg medially (52)	
51. Semitendinosus	Extends femur	
52. Popliteus	Flexes lower leg, rotates lower leg medially	
53. Plantaris	Plantar flexes foot (when knee is almost straight)	Quick starts in track, swimming, basketball, football, skating, all jumping, skiing
54. Gastrocnemius	Flexes lower leg	
55. Soleus	Plantar flexes foot	
56. Peroneus longus	Plantar flexes and everts foot	Changing directions while running, skating, skiing, running, all jumping, racing starts, skating turns
57. Peroneus brevis		

Muscle	Primary Action (numbers in parentheses indicate muscles that assist)	Sport in Which Greatest Resistance is Encountered
58. Extensor digitorum	Extends the four smaller toes	
59. Extensor hallicus	Extends the big toe	
60. Tibialis anterior	Dorsiflexes and inverts foot	
61. Tibialis posterior	Plantar flexes and inverts foot	
62. Flexor digitorum longus	Flexes the four smaller toes	
63. Flexor hallicus longus	Flexes the big toe	

Source: Adapted from Muscle Action Chart by Cramer Products, Inc. Reprinted by permission of Cramer Products, Inc., P.O. Box 1001, Gardner, KS 66030.

OVERLOAD PRINCIPLE

In any physical fitness program, the *overload principle* refers to the requirements necessary to bring about improvement in the various systems of the body. As the body is subject to loads greater than those to which the systems are accustomed, the various systems adjust and increase their capacity to perform physical work.

A classic example concerns the Greek hero Milo of Crotona. Each day Milo lifted a calf to his shoulders and ran through the stables. As the calf grew and added body weight, the increased weight provided the overload necessary to bring about the physiological changes in Milo's body systems to make him stronger. The same principle accounts for increased strength in any training program.

One contemporary example demonstrating the overload principle is the jogger who first runs only one mile and then each week adds another mile to the training program. Because of this overload, certain systems of the body are stimulated and increase their ability to perform the work of jogging. In time the jogger will easily be able to cover ten or more miles on a training run.

y systems require specific overloads. In jogging, for in-
ovascular system requires an overload that is different
necessary to bring about strength gains. This is referred
ecificity. The minimum resistance that a person can use
ent of obtaining strength gains is approximately 60 per-
um force that a muscle group can exert. The following
of the information necessary to ensure that the specific
......ad for strength will be contained in the planning of a strength training program.

BASIC DEFINITIONS

Before organizing a strength program, familiarity with the following defi-
nitions is necessary:

Accommodating resistance: the use of a machine that adjusts the
resistance in an attempt to obtain maximum resistance through a
full range of motion

Barbell: a bar with iron plates attached

Bodybuilder: a person who uses weight training to obtain a more
muscular physique; a physique athlete

Concentric contraction: a shortening of the muscle against resistance

Dumbbell: a hand weight

Dynamic action: muscle action with movement

Eccentric contraction: a lengthening of the muscle against resistance

Free weights: barbells and dumbbells; free weights differ from
strength training machines, which are restricted on how they can be
used

Isokinetic training: the use of a machine that controls the speed of
a muscle contraction and attempts to vary the resistance according
to the muscle force applied

Isometric action: muscle action without movement

Maximum resistance: maximum weight lifted in one repetition of
an exercise

Muscular endurance: the ability to perform repeated muscle movements for a given period of time

Periodization: dividing the training year into periods and manipulating the stress of training to combat overtraining

Physique: the body structure; organization or development of the physical appearance

Progressive resistance training: increasing the amount of weight lifted as one becomes stronger

Recovery period: the rest interval time between sets

Repetition maximum: the maximum amount of weight lifted for a given number of repetitions. For example, 1 RM would be the maximum weight lifted for one repetition, and 6 RM would be the maximum weight lifted for six repetitions

Repetitions: the number of times an exercise is performed

Set: a given number of repetitions

Strength: the ability to exert force against resistance

Variable resistance training: the use of a machine that adjusts the resistance through the range of movement of a muscle contraction to accommodate to the change in muscle strength at different joint angles

Weight lifting: competition that requires the participants to use specific lifts

Weight training: a systematic series of resistance exercises to develop strength

STRENGTH PROGRAMS

Strength development programs are basically either *dynamic* (muscle contractions with movement) or *isometric* (muscle contractions with little or no movement).

The most common type of training program is one using dynamic contractions. The major advantage of this system is that it brings about strength gains through a full range of motion. As a muscle goes through a range of motion, it must receive adequate resistance at all of the joint angles to stimulate strength increases. For example, if resistance is incurred at only the 90° angle, this is where the muscle will be stronger, not at the other angles, where resistance is not encountered. Dynamic training seems to have a greater effect on muscle hypertrophy, muscle endurance, increased flexibility, and development of connective tissue. This type of training also allows the individual to observe the work being done, which can be a source of satisfaction from a psychological standpoint.

From a cosmetic viewpoint, the gains made from a dynamic program are greater than those from an isometric program. Since many people engage in strength programs for body changes related to training, this is an added benefit for dynamic training.

Some advantages ascribed to an isometric training program are that it requires less equipment and usually causes little muscle soreness. This mode of training makes it possible to isolate specific joint angles to strengthen. In one program, specific isometric contractions with the leg muscles were used to increase the ability of various athletes to jump higher and farther. The primary training program, however, for the athletes was dynamic; isometric exercises were utilized to supplement this program.

A disadvantage of isometric training is that it causes high systolic and diastolic blood pressures, which might be harmful to the heart and circulatory system.

MACHINES VS. FREE WEIGHTS

In the past few years, as interest in the development of strength has increased, a dazzling array of exercise machines has appeared on the market. Advertisements use highly persuasive language to explain why their specific machines are best and why all other machines and training methods will soon be obsolete. Many advertisements contain testimonies from prominent athletes or coaches.

With the development of these machines have come new terms in strength training: *isokinetic* and *variable resistance*. As a muscle goes through a range of motion, the ability of the lever system to exert force changes at different angles. Thus the amount of weight that can be lifted is limited by the weakest point in the range of motion. Therefore many manufacturers of equipment have developed machines that theoretically have the ability to adjust the resistance of the machine to the muscle's ability to exert force. The claim is that these machines will bring about a faster and greater increase of strength through the full range of motion.

The other type of training devices are sometimes referred to as *free weights*. Free weights include barbells, dumbbells, and other related equipment. In the early 1900s, Allan Calvert developed adjustable barbells, with which weighted plates could be added or taken off to change the resistance. In over one hundred years, few changes have been made to alter his basic design.

Many discussions have taken place regarding the merits of machines versus free weights. Some observers believe that it is not an either-or problem; rather, a trainer should use many different methods in strength training. As long as the basic principles regarding strength development are observed, making strength gains and body changes with both machines and free weights is possible. Being consistent in your training in the program you choose is probably more important than the type of training device you select. The best recommendation is to experiment with different exercises and various types of training equipment and use them to develop a personalized program.

NUTRITION AND STRENGTH DEVELOPMENT

Nutrition affects virtually every function of the body. Nutrients from food are necessary for every heartbeat, nerve sensation, and muscle contraction.

Nutrients are chemical substances obtained from food during digestion. About fifty nutrients, including water, are needed daily for optimum health. No single substance will maintain good health. Although specific nutrients are known to have important functions in specific parts of the body, even those nutrients are dependent upon the presence of other nutrients for their best effects. An effort should be made to attain and maintain an adequate, balanced daily intake of all the necessary nutrients throughout life.

In 1992 the U.S. Department of Agriculture released what is called the Food Guide Pyramid. The purpose of this pyramid is to promote and symbolize a healthy diet for people in the United States. The foundation of the pyramid consists of breads, cereals, vegetables, and fruits. The Department of Agriculture believes that emphasizing these foods will put people well on the path to adequate and proper nutrition.

This guide has the advantages of simplicity and enough freedom of choice to fit individual preferences and different economic levels. Figure 2.10 describes the food groups and the servings necessary to provide a well-balanced diet.

Many times a person starting a strength training program becomes concerned about a need for extra protein in the diet. Hoping to increase body size and strength, many individuals have been attracted to high-protein diets and concentrated protein supplements. There is no scientific

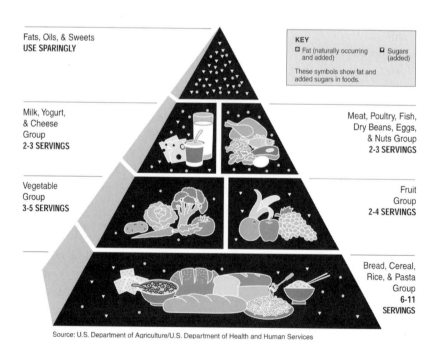

Figure 2.10 A Guide to Daily Food Choices

evidence that supports the belief that people engaging in strength programs require increased amounts of protein. The National Research Council recommends that both men and women consume one to two grams of protein per kilogram (2.2 lbs.) of body weight. The average American ingests two or three times as much protein as needed. Uncontrolled protein intake in the diet has some drawbacks. High-protein diets are dehydrating because they demand large amounts of water for urinary excretion of the metabolic by-products. Protein supplements may cause loss of appetite and diarrhea, and excess protein may also be changed to fat, stored in the body, and contribute to obesity.

The pyramid plan provides abundant protein and is the best nutritional program to follow for a training program.

GAINING BODY WEIGHT

Dr. Melvin Williams, the director of the Human Performance Laboratory at Old Dominion University, has developed excellent guidelines to help maximize gains in muscle tissue and keep body fat increases relatively low:

1. Set a reasonable goal within a certain time period. The greatest gains will be made in the first three months; in untrained young men, this can be approximately three pounds per month. In well-trained athletes and women, the gains will be much less. Gender and genetics are two of the major controlling factors in how much and how fast the lean body mass will be gained. After a few years of dietary intervention and training, the gains are reduced and may be limited to about 1 to 3 percent per year.
2. Increase your caloric intake. To add a pound of muscle tissue per week, you need to increase your caloric intake by approximately four hundred calories, and you need about fourteen grams of additional protein per day. One glass of skim milk, three slices of whole wheat bread, and two hard-boiled egg whites will provide the necessary calories and about twenty-three grams of protein.

    Many people assume that protein is the important food for increasing muscle mass, but total energy intake, primarily from carbohydrates, is what allows the body to train and to bring about the increased gain in muscle size. A more specific guideline for the total amount of protein needed is that an intake of one to two grams of protein per day for each 2.2 pounds of body weight will adequately meet the needs of a weight gain program.

3. Start a strength training exercise program. It is not the intake of food that provides the stimulus for increased muscle mass; rather, the use of the overload principle in a strength training program is what causes the muscles to increase in size.

4. Use a tape measure to take body measurements. Be sure to take them at the same place every one to two weeks. Body parts measured should include the neck, upper and lower arm, chest, abdomen, thigh, and calf. This measuring is to ensure that body weight gains are proportionately distributed. You should look for good gains in the chest and limbs, but the abdominal girth increase should be kept low because that is where fat usually increases the most. Appendix A contains a body measurement chart to record your measurements.

5. Beware of misleading information concerning dietary supplements that promise to effectively increase the amount of lean muscle mass. Many people who go on a weight gaining and strength training program have questions about the use of nutrition supplements. Table 2.3 contains information that will give you valid answers concerning the use of many of these so-called nutritional aids. As indicated, most advertised claims are speculative, since very little well-controlled research has been conducted for most of these purported nutritional supplements.

By following these suggestions, you can plan a program that will be very effective in gaining the proper kind of body weight.

ANABOLIC STEROIDS

Over the years individuals have taken anabolic steroids in an attempt to obtain increased muscle mass and strength. Steroids are artificial male hormones that have anabolic properties; that is, they cause a buildup of complex chemical units, such as muscle protein. There is much contradictory research as to whether the steroids accomplish their intended purpose. Anabolic steroids are banned by every international sports federation, and in some cases athletes have been banned from competition for using these drugs. The position statement that follows, from the American College of Sports Medicine, details some of the problems associated with their use. A person using anabolic steroids should consult first with a medical doctor and use them only under the doctor's supervision.

Based on a comprehensive survey of the world literature and a careful analysis of the claims made for and against the efficacy of anabolic-androgenic steroids in improving human physical performance, the position of the American College of Sports Medicine is as follows:

1. The administration of anabolic-androgenic steroids to healthy humans below age fifty in medically approved therapeutic doses often does not of itself bring about any significant improvements in strength, aerobic endurance, lean body mass, or body weight.
2. There is no conclusive scientific evidence that extremely large doses of anabolic-androgenic steroids either aid or hinder athletic performance.
3. The prolonged use of oral anabolic-androgenic steroids (C_{17}-alkylated derivatives of testosterone) has resulted in liver disorders in some persons. Some of these disorders are apparently reversible with the cessation of drug usage, but others are not.
4. The administration of anabolic-androgenic steroids to male humans may result in a decrease in testicular size and function and a decrease in sperm production. Although these effects appear to be reversible when small doses of steroids are used for short periods of time, the reversibility of the effects of large doses over extended periods of time is unclear.
5. Serious and continuing efforts should be made to educate male and female athletes, coaches, physical educators, physicians, trainers, and the general public regarding the inconsistent effects of anabolic-androgenic steroids on improvement of human physical performance and the potential dangers of taking certain forms of these substances, especially in large doses, for prolonged periods.

Table 2.3 Dietary Supplements Used by Athletes

Dietary Supplement	Claimed Benefits
Amino acids—branched chain *Leucine, isoleucine, valine*	❏ Increases endurance ❏ Postpones onset of fatigue ❏ Increases weight/strength ❏ Prevents muscle breakdown
Amino acids—individual *Building blocks of protein*	Arginine and ornithine ❏ Growth hormone releasers ❏ Decreases body fat ❏ Increases weight/muscle Tryptophan ❏ Relieves insomnia, depression, and PMS ❏ Increases growth hormone ❏ Enhances performance
Amino acids—mixtures *Partially digested proteins*	❏ Increases muscle mass ❏ Faster protein absorption
Aspartates *Organic salt*	❏ Increases energy ❏ Enhances fat metabolism ❏ Spares glycogen ❏ Postpones fatigue
Bicarbonates *Buffer*	❏ Facilitates performance in high-power events ❏ Decreases acid buildup that limits carbohydrate metabolism and induces fatigue

Efficacy	Safety/Other Concerns
❐ Appear to be metabolized at a higher rate during endurance exercise ❐ Research on the effects of supplementation on endurance performance is still elusive	❐ Safety thresholds of individual amino acids are not known
❐ Effects of arginine and ornithine remain to be proven; more research is warranted ❐ Tryptophan may have ergogenic benefits, but performance detriments (drowsiness, impaired glucose metabolism) and safety concerns have been shown ❐ Few performance-enhancing effects of individual amino acids have been proven	❐ Safety threshold of individual amino acids is not known; can pose serious risks to certain people: pregnant or nursing women, infants, children, adolescents, older adults, individuals with disorders in protein metabolism ❐ Tryptophan banned by FDA in 1990 due to reports of eosinophilia myalgia syndrome and resulting deaths
❐ No benefits for healthy adults with adequate protein intake ❐ Little evidence to support muscle gains	❐ Safety is questionable
❐ Research on benefits is inconclusive	❐ Small doses appear to pose minimal risk
❐ Conflicting evidence	❐ Can produce GI distress ❐ Banned by governing bodies of some sports

Continued.

Table 2.3 Continued

Dietary Supplement	Claimed Benefits
Boron *Nonessential trace mineral*	❏ Natural testosterone booster ❏ Increases weight/muscle
Caffeine *Central nervous system stimulant found in coffee, tea, chocolate, soft drinks, and over-the-counter drugs*	❏ Increases endurance performance ❏ Increases fat oxidation ❏ Increases motivation and postpones fatigue ❏ Increases short-term, intense exercise performance
Carnitine *Vitamin-like molecule synthesized from glutamate and methionine*	❏ Increases fatty acid oxidation (carbohydrate sparing) ❏ Fat loss (cutting) agent
Ciwujia *Chinese herb derived from root*	❏ Traditional Chinese medicine used to treat fatigue and boost immune function; used for 1,700 years ❏ Increases fat metabolism; spares glycogen ❏ Decreases lactic acid buildup ❏ Decreases heart rate
Choline *Precursor of neurotransmitter, acetylcholine; found in lecithin*	❏ Fat loss (cutting) agent ❏ Enhances endurance performance

Efficacy	Safety/Other Concerns
❐ A study on postmenopausal women showed increased testosterone levels with boron supplementation; effects on weight and muscle were not evaluated ❐ Inconclusive evidence	❐ Safety data not located
❐ Use of 3–6 mg/kg body weight can produce endurance benefits without adverse side effects or reaching illegal limits for sports competition ❐ Effects on short-term, intense exercise have not been well examined	❐ Can cause anxiety, jitters, GI discomfort, insomnia, irritability, and arrhythmias ❐ Wide variation of responses ❐ Diuretic effect of caffeine can promote dehydration ❐ Considered a "controlled or restricted substance" by IOC
❐ Benefits not substantiated ❐ No scientific basis to promote use by athletes	❐ Appears to be safe ❐ Large doses can cause diarrhea

❐ Chinese studies done on animals
❐ American studies have several design flaws:
  ❐ small number of subjects
  ❐ not double blind
  ❐ lack of controls
  ❐ subjects weren't athletes
  ❐ exercise was only of moderate intensity
  ❐ exercise ≤60 minutes
	❐ Manufacturer claims substance is remarkably safe
	❐ No other safety data located

❐ Effects on fat loss are largely theoretical ❐ Possible benefits in latter stages of endurance performance (greater than 15 miles), but more research is needed	❐ Nontoxic ❐ Large doses cause diarrhea ❐ Large doses emit a fishy smell

Continued.

Table 2.3 Continued

Dietary Supplement	Claimed Benefits
Chromium compounds (chromium piccolinate) *Essential trace mineral*	❐ Increases weight/muscle ❐ Insulin enhancer ❐ Increases glycogen stores ❐ Regulates fat deposition and decreases body fat
Coenzyme Q10 (CoQ10) *Type of fat found in mito-chondria*	❐ Increase oxygen uptake ❐ Increase exercise performance
Creatine *Substance involved in energy metabolism; cellu-lar component*	❐ Promotes phosphocreatine and ATP resynthesis during anaerobic work ❐ Enhances anaerobic performance ❐ Allows athlete to train longer at higher intensities without fatigue
Dibencozide *Cobalt-containing organic compound*	❐ Increases weight/muscle ❐ Active form of vitamin B12 ❐ Steroid alternative
Dessicated liver *Powder made from animal liver*	❐ Good source of protein, iron, zinc, and B vitamins ❐ Increases energy and endurance
Ferulic acid (ȳ-oryzanol) *Plant sterol*	❐ Increases weight/muscle ❐ Increases testosterone and growth hormone secretions ❐ Antioxidant ❐ Increases endorphins

Efficacy	Safety/Other Concerns
❏ Endurance exercise increases urinary losses of chromium ❏ Studies showing increases in muscle mass were poorly controlled ❏ Anabolic effects are inconclusive	❏ Estimated safe and adequate daily dietary intake is 50–200 micrograms/day ❏ Minimal risk of toxicity from oral supplementation
❏ Therapeutic use in cardiac patients shows promise ❏ Research on healthy athletes does not show same effects	❏ Safety data not located

❏ Shows promise
❏ More research needed to:
  ❏ substantiate benefits
  ❏ elucidate mechanisms
  ❏ establish safe/effective dosages
❏ Vegetarian athletes have lower creatine pool and are likely to benefit
	❏ Ingestion of 20 mg/day for 5 days appears to present minimal risk
	❏ Excesses excreted by kidneys

❏ No substantiation for anabolic benefits ❏ Cobalamin is the active form of B12	❏ Safety data not located
❏ Effects small in context of total diet	❏ Safety data not located
❏ Based on anecdotal evidence ❏ No controlled research to support anabolic claims ❏ Metabolized in GI tract, poorly absorbed, does not enter bloodstream intact ❏ Endorphin effect may have some basis, but more research is needed	❏ Low toxicity ❏ Individuals with lipid storage disease may get xanthomatosis (nodular yellowish fat deposits around eyelids and on hands)

Continued.

Table 2.3 Continued

Dietary Supplement	Claimed Benefits
Ginseng *Extract of ginseng root*	❐ Protects against tissue damage ❐ Decreases lactate buildup ❐ Increases VO_{2max}
Inosine *Nucleoside, substance involved in energy metabolism*	❐ Activates cellular function ❐ Enhances endurance ❐ Stimulates ATP production; aids exercise intensity ❐ Promotes strength
Ma huang (squaw tea, Mormon tea, ephedra) *Herbal supplement*	❐ Controls weight ❐ Boosts energy
Medium chain triglycerides (MTC) *Short fat molecules which are more readily absorbed*	❐ Increases energy ❐ Decreases body fat ❐ Increases muscle ❐ Enhances metabolism and extends endurance ❐ Decreases serum cholesterol
Pangamic acid (calcium pangamate, vitamin B15) *Organic chemical*	❐ Increase muscle glycogen ❐ Enhance aerobic metabolism ❐ Vitamin essential to health

Efficacy	Safety/Other Concerns
❏ Conflicting evidence	❏ High doses cause elevated blood pressure, nervousness, and confusion
❏ Minimal supporting evidence from rat studies; human studies refute claim ❏ Some studies show impaired performance ❏ Does not appear to be an effective ergogenic aid	❏ Uric acid is by-product, so individuals with predisposition to gout and kidney stones should avoid inosine
	❏ Numerous reports of adverse effects: liver failure, elevated blood pressure, palpitations, strokes ❏ 20 documented deaths ❏ When combined with caffeine, raises potential for harmful effects ❏ IOC bans use of ephedra
❏ Effective for people with malabsorption disorders ❏ Effectiveness in athletes not documented	❏ Not safe for people with liver disease and diabetes
❏ Claims based on animal studies from Soviet Union ❏ Several well-controlled studies in U.S. have showed no effect on cardiovascular and metabolic responses to exercise ❏ No essentiality to human nutrition established	❏ FDA-approved additive with no margin of safety

Continued.

Table 2.3 Continued

Dietary Supplement	Claimed Benefits
Phosphate salts *Buffer*	❏ Facilitates performance in high-power events ❏ Decreases acid buildup that limits carbohydrate metabolism and induces fatigue ❏ Stimulates carbohydrate metabolism and enhances anaerobic performance
Sarsparilla (Smilax) *Plant sterol*	❏ Increases weight/muscle ❏ Natural form of testosterone
Yohimbe (yohimbine) *Tree bark containing druglike chemicals*	❏ Aphrodisiac ❏ Treatment for impotence ❏ Natural testosterone

Source: Adapted from Jean Starlie, "A Strategy for Supplements," Training and Conditioning 7, no. 4 (August 1997). Reprinted with permission of publisher.
Note: The literature reviewed to compile this table did not discuss the safety of numerous supplements. Other sources were consulted, but in several cases data could not be located.

Efficacy	Safety/Other Concerns
❐ Inconclusive evidence	❐ Low doses appear to pose minimal risk ❐ Some people experience gastrointestinal distress
❐ Based on practices of early Central American Indians ❐ No supporting research	❐ Safety data not located
❐ Effectiveness unknown and questionable	❐ Serious adverse effects reported: kidney failure, seizures, and death ❐ Side effects include anxiety attacks, elevated blood pressure ❐ Serious adverse interactions when taken with liver, cheese, red wine and some over-the-counter-drugs (e.g., decongestants)

Variables in a Strength Training Program

CHAPTER 3

A well-designed program to develop strength and reduce the chance of injury must take into consideration the following variables:

1. Resistance to utilize
2. Number of repetitions
3. Number of sets
4. Rest interval between sets
5. Frequency of workouts during the week
6. Safety procedures

A systematic overloading of a muscle increases the strength and size of the muscle. Four possible methods can be used to increase the difficulty of a strength workout:

1. Increase the resistance
2. Increase the repetitions
3. Increase the number of sets
4. Decrease the time of the rest intervals between sets

RESISTANCE

The greatest strength gains seem to be obtained when the resistance is increased and the other variables are held constant. The *minimum* resistance that can be used and still get strength gains is approximately 60 percent of the maximum force or weight lifted for one muscle contraction. The maximum force that can be exerted is referred to as the 1 RM.

It might appear that the fastest way to obtain strength would be to do exercises that require a single repetition of maximum force. However, the problem with this type of training is that it may cause injury to the muscle or connective tissue. It may also lead to chronic fatigue of the muscle and retard the progress toward increased strength and muscle development.

Since it is difficult to determine exactly how much weight a person should be lifting for each exercise, some guidelines are needed. Through the years the "guesstimate" method of determining resistance has been utilized with great success. This method has been used with both beginning weight training classes and elite athletes. The process is one of trial and error.

1. Guess how many pounds you can lift for a specific exercise.
2. Try this weight for the given number of repetitions for one set, i.e., 6 RM, 10 RM, and so on.
3. If the exercise is too easy and you can do more than the recommended number of repetitions, increase the resistance for the next set.
4. If the exercise is too hard and you cannot do the recommended number of repetitions, decrease the resistance for the next set.
5. Remember to increase the weight for the next workout whenever you can do more than the recommended number of repetitions on the last set of an exercise.

REPETITIONS

Resistance exceeding 60 percent of maximum has been found to be very effective in bringing about strength gains in a training program. When you use between 5 and 12 RM, over 70 percent of the repetitions will be above 60 percent of the 1 RM and will thus ensure that you are obtaining a proper training stimulus. A rule of thumb that works well in determining the weight load to use in an exercise is as follows:

If your objective is increased muscle strength then decrease the repetitions, increase the resistance.

If your objective is increased muscle endurance then increase the repetitions, decrease the resistance.

Thus a football player who wishes a greater increase in strength might use 5 RM, and a long-distance runner who needs muscle endurance might use 15 RM.

SETS

The most popular and versatile system of strength development is the set system, in which an individual performs an exercise for a given number of repetitions, rests for an interval of time, and repeats the exercise for a given number of sets. This system can be adapted to any objective in strength development for the beginner, the bodybuilder, the athlete, or the advanced weight lifter.

Most beginning weight trainers make good progress by using a program consisting of three or four sets using 6 to 10 RM in each set.

ONE SET ONLY

The excuse that many people use for not exercising is that they don't have enough time. For instance, ten different exercises for three sets and ten repetitions with a two-minute recovery between each set would take approximately ninety minutes. If you did only one set of ten different exercises and went from one body part to the next without a recovery, then the workout time could be reduced to less than twenty minutes—certainly a reasonable amount of time to be allotted to strength training. Research studies have shown that one set of 6 to 10 RM is effective for providing a strength stimulus that will produce significant strength gains.

People who train on Nautilus machines are recommended to do only one set of 8 to 12 RM. Olympic weight lifters and power lifters often train using five to ten sets of 1 to 5 RM each set. Bodybuilders may utilize five to ten sets of 10 to 15 RM in their workouts.

If a major goal is to increase muscle mass, the volume of the workout (sets and repetitions) may need to be increased. There is a relationship between increased hypertrophy and increased volume. The following are some of the reasons that are thought to influence this relationship:

1. Increased volume may stimulate the activation of a maximum number of muscle cells and increase the tension being placed on the contractile fibrils.
2. Increased volume may cause an increase in the secretion of anabolic hormones, which are some of the chemical modulators that stimulate the growth of muscle tissue.
3. Increased volume may cause the muscle cell to use an energy-releasing system (anaerobic glycolysis) that produces lactic acid. An accumula-

tion of lactic acid may promote an increase in the production of anabolic hormones such as testosterone and growth hormone.

4. Increased volume may augment myofibrilar hydration, or the "muscle pump," which may stimulate protein synthesis and inhibit protein breakdown in the muscle cell. For a full explanation of the "muscle pump," go to page 167.

If your goal is to increase muscle mass, then you might do multiple exercises with three to five sets of eight to twelve repetitions with a two-minute recovery between sets. For example, you might do three different exercises for the biceps of the arm using four sets per exercise and ten repetitions per set. The chapter on bodybuilding provides examples of various training routines that might be utilized to manipulate the volume to obtain increased muscle hypertrophy.

Each exercise should commence with a warm-up set of a lighter weight. A set of ten repetitions using 50 percent of the maximum weight that can be lifted works very well as a warm-up set. This will help to reduce injury and prepare the muscle system for additional resistance in the following sets.

REST INTERVAL BETWEEN SETS

The rest interval between sets is an important consideration in designing a strength training program. The amount of time taken between sets is determined by individual training objectives. For example, bodybuilders usually take very short rest periods, while weight lifters and athletes training with near to maximum weight loads require relatively extended rest periods between sets.

One way to determine the rest interval is to be aware of the primary energy sources required in the lifting of weights. This energy source, which is composed of the chemicals adenosine triphosphate and phosphocreatine, is known as the *phosphagen stores*. These phosphagen stores have the ability to provide maximum energy for short periods of time and usually last for no more than ten seconds.

These stores are quickly replenished in the rest interval. Within thirty seconds, approximately 50 percent of the phosphagens are resynthesized and available for another bout of exercise. Table 3.1 shows the amount of rest time and the approximate percentage of phosphagen stores replenished.

Table 3.1 Replenishment of Phosphagen Stores

Rest Time	Approximate Percentage of Phosphagen Stores Replenished
0 seconds	0.00
30 seconds	50.00
60 seconds (1 minute)	75.00
90 seconds	87.50
120 seconds (2 minutes)	93.75
150 seconds	96.88
180 seconds (3 minutes)	98.44
210 seconds	99.22
240 seconds (4 minutes)	99.61
270 seconds	99.80
300 seconds (5 minutes)	99.90

As indicated by table 3.1, most of the phosphagen stores are replenished within two minutes. Individuals, such as bodybuilders, who wish to obtain the so-called muscle pump, might use one-minute intervals. Those who are lifting near-maximum weight would increase the rest interval to three or more minutes. In most cases, a rest interval of approximately two minutes should be an adequate amount of time.

The recovery is specific to the muscles involved in the exercise. To reduce the time necessary to complete a workout, one could alternate sets of different exercises. For example, do a set using the chest muscles, such as the bench press, and a set utilizing the legs, such as the leg press. Do the exercises until the required number of sets is completed, and then you can move on to two different exercises.

WORKOUT FREQUENCY

When the body systems, such as the muscular system, are overloaded, cells require a certain amount of time to recover and undergo the physiological changes that are involved in training. If the recovery time is too short, the muscle cells are unable to accommodate and rebuild to ensure a higher level of strength. This can lead to chronic fatigue and may even result in a loss of strength. A decrease in performance is the best indicator that a person needs more rest and a decrease in work.

Most strength workouts require a rest day between each workout day for the various muscle groups exercised. A muscle group should be trained on three nonconsecutive days each week, such as Monday, Wednesday, and Friday. In chapter 7, Bodybuilding and Physique Training, a type of training known as the split-body routine is explained. Using this routine, a person can work out every day by exercising one part of the body one day, then letting it rest while training another body part on the next day.

A person can train any time during the day. Training time is usually determined by the amount of time available and when training facilities can be used.

AMERICAN COLLEGE OF SPORTS MEDICINE GUIDELINES

The American College of Sports Medicine makes the following recommendations, which apply to exercises for individuals at all levels. These suggestions will be helpful in obtaining good results with strength training.

1. Strength training exercises should involve both eccentric and concentric actions.
2. Exercises should involve single joints and multiple joints for beginners, intermediates, and advanced lifters. When maximum power output is the goal, a majority of the exercises should involve mostly multiple-joint lifts.
3. Exercise large muscle groups before small muscle groups, multiple-joint exercises before single-joint exercises, and high-intensity exercises before those of lower intensity.
4. Generally, the order of exercises should be from large to small, from multiple-joint exercise to single-joint, from high intensity to low intensity, and from most complex to least complex.
5. Periodization, which is explained in chapter 6, allows the strength trainer to use variety in sequencing exercises.

SAFETY PROCEDURES

An examination of the accidents in various activities reveals that weight training is one of the safest forms of recreation a person can participate in. However, some common sense rules should be followed.

If a person has been sedentary for a long period and suspects some medical problem, a good physical examination by a qualified physician would be wise.

Frederick C. Hatfield and March L. Krotee, in their book *Personalized Weight Training for Fitness and Athletics: From Theory to Practice,* have compiled a list of recommended guidelines that is excellent advice for any weight trainer:

1. Never train alone. Injuries and accidents can often be avoided when someone else is present. It's also more fun to involve others as either a primary or secondary partner. A weight training room should be supervised by trained personnel.
2. Inspect equipment, read instructions, and have a qualified instructor demonstrate each piece of equipment. In short, if you don't know what you're doing, seek professional advice and guidance. Your chances of reaching your training aims and objectives will be greatly enhanced.
3. Use experienced spotters whenever necessary. Heavy squats and bench presses are especially dangerous, and under no circumstances should they be attempted without one or two knowledgeable spotters. Other exercises such as good mornings, hyperextensions, and incline or decline presses also require spotting.
4. Keep alert and lift weights or engage in associated physical activity in designated areas only. With multiuse equipment, be aware of where you are as well as the location of others around you. Be careful not to walk directly in front of lifters, as you may startle them, disturb their concentration, or even inadvertently bump into their equipment.
5. Always check your weights and immediate training environment before each set. Be sure that even loading is followed, collars are tightened, and barbell sleeves are free to revolve. Count your weight!
6. Use equipment as it was designed to be employed. Improper use can cause injury, equipment breakdowns, and lost training time.
7. Keep lifting and exercise areas clean, neat, and orderly. Place weights in designated areas after using, as misplaced weights are often the cause of injury.
8. When using weight training machines, carefully check all cables, pulleys, selector keys (use appropriate key, not a substitute), nuts, bolts, cam chains, seat adjustments, and belts for maximum safety. The equipment should also be kept clean and appropriately lubricated. If equipment jams, do not attempt to free it yourself. Report all problems immediately to the weight training supervisor.

9. Wear proper lifting attire and remember that perspiration causes slippery equipment and skin—both dangerous conditions. Don't lift in your stocking feet.

10. Use proper breathing techniques when lifting. If a person takes a deep breath and holds it while straining to lift the weight, this can significantly decrease the blood flow to an area of the body. The increased pressure in the chest cavity that can result when holding the breath can hinder the venous blood return to the heart and elevate blood pressure. This is known as the *Valsalva effect.*

    To assure that you have proper breathing procedures in strength training:

    a. Remove the bar from the rack or apply pressure to the resistance lever if using a machine and stabilize the weight.
    b. Inspire deeply, thus stabilizing the appropriate body structures.
    c. Lower the weight (eccentric action).
    d. Raise the weight (concentric action) and expire during the last one-half to two-thirds of the upward movement.
    e. Repeat the cycle.
    f. Always keep the mouth open.

11. Don't lift if an injury may be aggravated. Temporarily modify the activity to exclude the injured area or associated muscle group.

12. If you're not feeling well or even up to par, you should temporarily suspend lifting. When recovering from an illness, resume lifting at a level of intensity and weight level well below that achieved before the illness.

13. Attend to weight training through a planned personalized program of progressive resistance training. This will reduce muscle soreness and aching joints and tendons, and will reduce your chance for injury. Proper technique and supervision in a professionally developed weight training program are mandatory.

14. Be aware of environmental conditions such as room temperature, humidity, altitude, and pollution count, and adapt your weight lifting program accordingly.

15. Don't lift immediately after a heavy meal.

16. Excessively hot showers should be avoided immediately after training. In some rare instances, hot showers have been associated with manifestations of myocardial infarction or heart attack.

17. Weight training does not have to be highly competitive in nature to be healthful. In fact, spontaneous and unwarranted 1 RMs, such as trying to outlift a colleague, often leads to a loss of safety focus concerning the physiological boundaries for safe participation.

18. As part of the physiological and psychological preparation for weight training, the warm-up may be considered a safety precaution. Warm-up is a preparation that is conducted at submaximal effort for a duration of approximately five to fifteen minutes immediately before engaging in lifting. Warm-up should be intense enough to increase body temperature and cause perspiration, but should not require a longer duration of submaximal effort. The value of warm-up seems to be quite controversial for participation in various sport specific situations; however, for the individual engaging in regular, vigorous weight training, warm-up is deemed a vital safety factor.

WEIGHT LIFTING BELTS

Weight lifting belts have been used for many years. The purpose of the belt is to add support to the lumbar spine and lower back during heavy lifts. Research indicates that using a belt may bring about an increase in intra-abdominal pressure. This increase in pressure allows all of the contents within the abdominal cavity to share compression loads that might otherwise have a negative effect on the spine.

If the goal is to lift the maximum amount of weight possible or to do a given exercise to complete fatigue, then the use of a weight lifting belt might be beneficial. Using a belt might bring about a 5 to 15 percent increase in the amount of weight lifted in such exercises as the squat, dead lift, and power clean. Some research indicates that weight lifting belts may delay the onset of fatigue when doing many repetitions in the squat by adding support to the body.

Using weight lifting belts can have disadvantages as well. Doing maximum lifts or lifting to exhaustion might increase the probability of injury. Training to failure is not necessary for strength development. When you use a weight lifting belt, supporting muscles that can cause increased intra-abdominal pressure might do the opposite of what you want them to do. The muscles push against the belt to increase pressure, but during times of high force production when you are not using a belt, you want the muscles to contract and pull in to increase intra-abdominal pressure. When the time comes to produce a large amount of force without a belt, the intra-abdominal pressure drops, which leaves the spine unprotected, increasing the chance of injury. Also, the use of a belt may strain the cardiovascular system by increasing blood pressure.

The natural supporting musculature of the body can also increase intra-abdominal pressure and protect the spine and lumbar regions. By using a belt, the core musculature of the body may not receive the necessary training stimulus, especially for strengthening the abdominal muscles. By doing strength exercises without a belt, all of the various muscle groups utilized in a given lift can be stimulated without relying on the support of the belt.

Using a belt is primarily beneficial when a person is training for a sport that requires maximal lifts. Never put the back at risk for injury if there are no performance gains to be made.

A weight lifting belt might be useful in protecting the back during periods of rehabilitation. During this time, you should not attempt maximum lifts but should be training to strengthen the entire body without risking further injury to the back.

The final decision on the use of belts can be made by answering the questions "What is the final goal of the program?" and "What is the person who is exercising trying to accomplish?"

DELAYED ONSET MUSCLE SORENESS

Many people, regardless of their fitness level, experience muscle soreness after engaging in strenuous exercise or at the beginning of a new exercise program. Many times the soreness and stiffness are not felt until twenty-four to forty-eight hours after the completion of the exercise. This type of muscle soreness is referred to as *delayed onset muscle soreness* (DOMS).

Physiological research reveals that the primary cause of DOMS is the overloading of a muscle during the eccentric (lengthening) portion of the movement. Greater tension can be generated during an eccentric action compared with either a concentric (shortening) or isometric (no movement) action. Thus the muscle cells become more susceptible to structural damage. This damage can lead to muscle soreness, decreased range of motion of the joint-lever system, a loss of strength, and a possible decrease in neuromuscular function.

Ways to prevent or lessen the effects of DOMS are as follows:

Warm-up: Warming up before an exercise prepares the body to exercise. Research data indicates that proper warm-up before eccentric exercise may be a sound method to alleviate DOMS. Using a warm-up set of lower resistance for each strength exercise will in most cases be very beneficial.

Repeated Bout Effect: Research has found that the musculature will adjust to the stress of exercise and become less susceptible to damage. One study found that even after one exercise bout, the inflammatory response to muscle damage was lessened when compared with engaging in the second bout of activity. It may be that the muscle cells become slightly longer so that the effects of the eccentric actions are less damaging. Another possibility is that the nervous system becomes more efficient in activating the muscle, which relieves the amount of stress on the active motor units.

The repeated bout effect can be facilitated when the first bout of exercise is only of a moderate intensity. If you engage in a program that produces little DOMS, an adaptation of the body will begin and the training process will be positive. In any strength training program you should start gradually and not make large increases in the overload of the selected exercises. Even well-trained individuals will develop DOMS if they make dramatically large increases or change the workout without a gradual adjustment to the program.

Body Measurements and Record Keeping

CHAPTER 4

Attempting to reach the goal of strength development can be compared to taking a journey. If you are planning a trip, you need to know where you are starting from and how many miles you have traveled.

By taking your body measurements when you start your program, you will have a means to determine the progress you are making. Record keeping will enable you to evaluate how well the body responds to specific exercises and thus make any changes that might be beneficial to your individual needs. As you compare the increases in resistance used in the various exercises, you also will have a means to determine the strength gains being made by selected body parts.

TAKING MEASUREMENTS

One of the simplest methods to monitor change is to measure the circumference of selected body parts with a tape. When taking measurements, keep the tape firm, but do not apply enough pressure to make indentations in the skin. By following this procedure, you will have measurements that are reliable and indicate structural changes. All the measurements should be taken in a standing position. In some cases you may wish to take two sets of measurements, one with the body part relaxed and a second with the body part in a flexed position.

Following are some standardized procedures to follow in measuring selected body parts. Figure 4.1 can be used to record the body measurements.

Name _____ Age _____

Date											
Body Weight											
Neck											
Shoulders											
Chest — Relaxed											
Chest — Flexed											
Upper Arm											
Relaxed — Right											
Relaxed — Left											
Flexed — Right											
Flexed — Left											
Forearm											
Relaxed — Right											
Relaxed — Left											
Flexed — Right											
Flexed — Left											
Waist											
Hips											
Thigh											
Relaxed — Right											
Relaxed — Left											
Flexed — Right											
Flexed — Left											
Calf											
Relaxed — Right											
Relaxed — Left											
Flexed — Right											
Flexed — Left											
Other Body Parts											

Figure 4.1 Body Measurement Chart

Neck—measure at the smallest circumference when relaxed.

Shoulders—measure the circumference at the greatest width.

Chest—*relaxed,* measure at greatest circumference after exhaling; *flexed,* measure at greatest circumference after inhaling.

Upper Arm—*relaxed,* measure at largest circumference with arm hanging; *flexed,* measure at largest circumference with elbow at a 90° angle.

Forearm—*relaxed,* measure largest circumference with arm hanging; *flexed,* measure largest circumference while flexing muscles by bending the elbow and the wrist.

Waist—measure at smallest circumference after exhaling.

Hips—measure at largest circumference.

Thigh—*relaxed,* measure the largest circumference; *flexed,* measure the largest circumference while straightening the leg and contracting the thigh muscles.

Calf—*relaxed,* measure the largest circumference; *flexed,* measure the largest circumference while contracting the muscles of the lower leg by raising the heel.

STRENGTH TEST

Although it may be impossible to determine the exact amount of force a given muscle group may exert, it is possible to estimate strength fitness rating by a series of strength tests. This information can be helpful in determining some body areas that might require more exercises to bring about positive results. Figure 4.2 contains the information and procedures to follow to complete the strength test.

STRENGTH TRAINING RECORD

Compiling a strength training record can also be a tremendous aid in your program. This record enables you to know the exercises you are using and the exact poundage to lift for that exercise. By comparing the various exercise days, you can easily determine how much improvement you have made at any given time. Figure 4.3 is an example of a strength training record.

Name _____

PROCEDURES FOR ADMINISTERING STRENGTH TEST

1. Familiarize yourself with the six exercises utilized for the test.
   a. Lat Pull-down (LPD)—Start in a seated position and have someone hold the subject down at the shoulders. (page 111)
   b. Leg Extension (LE) (page 135)
   c. Bench Press (BP) (page 103)
   d. Curl-Up (CU)—Hold the weight on the front of the forehead, keep the knees flexed at a 100° angle, and have someone hold the feet. Curl forward and touch the elbows to the knees. (page 121)
   e. Leg Curl (LC)—flex the knee until the subject reaches a 90° angle. (page 148)
   f. Arm Curl (AC) (page 75)
2. Determine subject's weight in pounds.
3. Determine the amount of resistance to be used for each exercise. To obtain this number, multiply the body weight by the percentage of body weight given for each exercise in the chart at the bottom of the worksheet. Round the number to the lowest five pounds. For example, 54 is rounded to 50.
4. Record your resistance in the bottom of the worksheet.
5. Perform the maximum continuous number of repetitions for each exercise.
6. Determine the percentile rank for each exercise.

Strength Test

Men							Women						
% Rank	LPD	LE	BP	CU	LC	AC	% Rank	LPD	LE	BP	CU	LC	AC
90	19	19	19	23	19	19	90	21	18	20	22	12	20
80	16	15	16	17	15	15	80	16	13	16	14	10	16
70	13	14	13	14	13	12	70	13	11	13	11	9	14
60	11	13	11	12	11	10	60	11	10	11	6	7	12
50	10	12	10	10	10	9	50	10	9	10	5	6	10
40	9	10	7	8	8	8	40	9	8	5	4	5	8
30	7	9	5	5	6	7	30	7	7	3	2	4	7
20	6	7	3	3	4	5	20	6	5	1	1	3	6
10	4	5	1	2	3	3	10	3	3	0	0	1	3
5	3	3	0	1	1	2	5	2	1	0	0	0	2

Figure 4.2 Strength Test

7. Determine the strength category and number of points for each exercise.

% Rank	90	80–89	60–79	40–59	20–39	10–19	less than 10
Strength Category	Superior	Excellent	Good	Average	Fair	Poor	Very Poor
Points	19	17	15	13	11	9	7

8. Record percentile rank, strength category, and number of points below.

Exercise	% Body Weight Men	Women	Resistance	Reps	% Rank	Strength Category	Pts
1. Lat Pull-Down	.70	.45					
2. Leg Extension	.65	.50					
3. Bench Press	.75	.45					
4. Curl-Up	.16	.10					
5. Leg Curl	.32	.25					
6. Arm Curl	.35	.18					

Total Points

Figure 4.2 Continued

Name _____ Age _____

Date					
Exercise	Wt Reps	Wt Reps	Wt Reps	Wt Reps	Wt Reps

Figure 4.3 Strength Training Record

THE SPORT EXPERIENCE

Use the body measurement chart, strength test, and strength training record to record your information at the start of your strength training program. After you have engaged in your training program for three or more months, take all of these measurements again to determine how your body is changing. Additional body measurement charts, strength tests, and strength training records can be found in Appendices A, B, and C.

Planning
the Strength
Training
Program

CHAPTER 5

In planning a strength training program to ensure overall body strength and development, six major body parts should be included:

1. Neck
2. Arms (biceps, triceps, wrists, and shoulders)
3. Chest
4. Back
5. Midsection
6. Legs

When designing the program, the individual must be aware of the equipment available and the amount of training time that he or she has. The desired outcomes to be achieved by the program should also be known.

At the end of this chapter are descriptions of the various exercises that can be employed. Photographs show the exercise, followed by an explanation concerning the starting position of the exercise, the action to be followed, and any precautions to be aware of while doing the exercise.

Table 5.1 lists the six major body parts and the exercises that will strengthen the muscles in these body parts. By using this table you can select exercises to develop any part of the body. Please note that although an exercise is listed under one area, as the bench press is under the chest area, it will also involve other parts of the body such as the arms.

You can now design a program using one or more exercises per body part. Following is an example of a beginning strength training program

Table 5.1 Weight Training Exercises

Body Part	Exercise	Sets	Repetitions	Rest Interval
Chest	Bench Press	3	10 RM	2 minutes
Midsection	Curl-up	3	30 RM	2 minutes
Triceps	Triceps press-down	3	10 RM	2 minutes
Legs	Leg press	3	10 RM	2 minutes
Shoulders	Dips	3	10 RM	2 minutes
Neck	Partner resistance	3	10 RM	2 minutes
Biceps	Arm curl	3	10 RM	2 minutes
Legs	Leg curl	3	10 RM	2 minutes
Back	Lat pull-down	3	10 RM	2 minutes
Wrists	Wrist curl	3	10 RM	2 minutes

that will develop overall body strength. The resistance to be used in this program would be determined by using the "guesstimate" method, which was explained in chapter 3.

Note that the rest period for each exercise is two minutes. If you find that the time allotted for strength training is too short to do all of the exercises, then an excellent routine to follow is to alternate the selected exercises in groups of two rather than taking a rest period. For example, first you do one set of the bench press and then one set of curl-ups, then do another set of the bench press and a second set of curl-ups, and so on. You combine exercises 1 and 2, 3 and 4, 5 and 6, 7 and 8, and 9 and 10. Since you are using different muscle groups, recovery can take place in the nonexercising muscle group while you are training the exercising muscle group.

As explained in chapter 3, it is possible to obtain strength gains by using one set for each exercise and not having a recovery period between each of the exercises. This is another way to reduce the time needed for a strength training program.

THE SPORT EXPERIENCE

Write a beginning strength training program for yourself using the strength training worksheet found in Appendix D.

STRENGTH TRAINING EXERCISES

Recall that the overload principle is what brings about the desired changes in a strength training program, not the training device utilized in the program. For example, if you do an arm curl with either free weights or a machine and use the proper overload, you will obtain a training effect.

The majority of the exercise photographs were taken using free weights to provide the resistance. If you are using a machine in your training, make sure the resistance is applied to the lever arm and is of a high enough amount.

NECK

NECK STRAP

Starting Position: Place the strap on the head, and take a seated position on the bench.

Action:
A. Muscles on the back of the neck: Bend over slightly at the waist, and move the head forward and backward. Allow the weight to hang between the legs.
B. Muscle on the front of the neck: Bend slightly backward, and move the head forward and backward. Allow the weight to hang behind the back.
C. Muscles on the side of the neck: Lean slightly to the right, and move the head from side to side. Allow the weight to hang to the right side of the body. When you have completed the desired number of repetitions, move the weight to the left side of the body and repeat the exercise.

Precautions: Since the neck muscles are usually quite weak, start with higher repetitions and light weights. Do not jerk the weight or use unnecessary body motion in the movement.

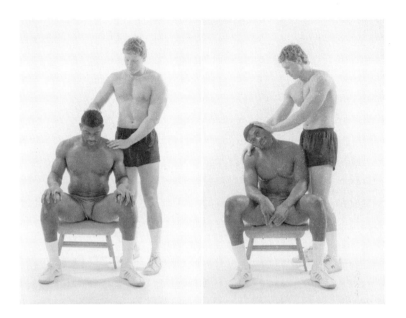

Partner Resistance

Starting Position: Take a seated position on the bench.

Action: To provide resistance, the partner pushes against the head as the neck muscles contract in the various positions: forward, backward, and sideways.

Precautions: Be sure to exercise all the neck muscles. Do not jerk the head in the movement.

Wrestler's Bridge

Starting Position: Lie flat on your back with your head resting on a pad. Pull the feet in close to the buttocks until the weight of the body is supported by the head and the feet.

Action: Rotate the body on the head using a forward and backward and side-to-side motion.

Precautions: Do not use a jerky movement.

Note: To increase the resistance, weights can be placed on the chest or a partner can push against the chest while the exercise is done.

BICEPS

Arm Curl

Starting Position: Grasp the bar about the width of the shoulders using a palms-up grip. The arms are extended, and the bar rests against the thighs.

Action: Curl the bar up to the shoulder area. Touch, and then return to the starting position.

Precautions: The elbows should be kept close to the sides of the body. Keep the body erect with the head up. Avoid any unnecessary body movement.

Reverse Curl

Starting Position: Grasp the bar about the width of the shoulders using a palms-down grip. The arms are extended, and the bar rests against the thighs.

Action: Curl the bar up to the shoulder area. Touch, and then return to the starting position.

Precautions: The elbows should be kept close to the sides of the body. Keep the body erect with the head up. Avoid any unnecessary body movement.

PREACHER-BOARD CURL

Starting Position: Adjust the stand to a height where you can place your arms over the angled padding with the back of the arms resting on the pad. Grasp the bar about the width of the shoulders using a palms-up grip.

Action: Curl the bar up to the shoulder area. Touch, and then return to the starting position.

Precautions: Do not jerk the weight, and avoid any unnecessary body movement.

DUMBBELL CURL

Starting Position: Stand erect with the feet about shoulder width. Grasp the dumbbells with a palms-up grip with the arms fully extended.

Action: Curl the dumbbells until they reach the top of the shoulders. Touch and return to the starting position.

Precautions: Keep the elbows close to the body. Do not jerk or use any unnecessary motion in the movement.

NOTE: This exercise can be performed in a seated position and can also be done by alternating one arm then the other in the curling movement.

INCLINE DUMBBELL CURL

Starting Position: Lie on an incline board while grasping the dumb-bells in a palms-up grip. The arms are extended with the head and back against the board.

Action: Curl the dumbbells until they reach the shoulders. Touch, and return to the starting position.

Precautions: Do not arch the back or use the legs in the movement. Do not jerk the weight to start the motion.

DUMBBELL CONCENTRATION CURL

Starting Position: Take a seated position on the bench. Grasp the dumbbell in the palms-up grip, and place the elbow on the inside of the right thigh to stabilize the upper arm. The arm is fully extended. The left hand is placed on the left thigh for support.

Action: Curl the dumbbell to the shoulder. Touch, and return to the starting position. After completing the desired number of repetitions, change the dumbbell to the left hand to complete the exercise for both arms.

Precautions: Keep the upper torso and legs stationary during the exercise. Do not jerk the dumbbell, and avoid any unnecessary motion during the movement.

SUPINE CURL

Starting Position: Lie on the bench with the feet flat on the floor. Grasp the dumbbells with a palms-up grip. The arms are extended from the sides of the body toward the floor.

Action: Curl the dumbbells to the shoulders. Touch, and return to the starting position.

Precautions: Do not arch the back or use any unnecessary motion during the movement.

TRICEPS

STANDING OVERHEAD PRESS

Starting Position: Stand erect with the feet shoulder width apart. The head is up with the eyes facing straight ahead. The bar rests at the midline of the chest; a palms-up grip is used.

Action: Push the bar overhead until the arms are fully extended. Lower the bar to the starting position.

Precautions: Keep the head up and the back straight. Do not bend the knees to assist the upper-body muscles in the movement.

SEATED OVERHEAD PRESS

Starting Position: Take a seat on the bench with the feet flat on the floor. Use a palms-up grip with the bar placed at the top of the chest. The head is up and the back straight.

Action: Push the bar overhead until the arms are fully extended. Return to the starting position.

Precautions: Do not jerk the weight or use any unnecessary body motion in the movement.

BEHIND-NECK PRESS

Starting Position: Stand erect with the feet shoulder width apart. The head is up with the eyes facing straight ahead. The bar is behind the neck and across the shoulders and held with an overhand grip.

Action: Push the bar overhead until the arms are fully extended. Lower the bar to the starting position.

Precautions: Keep the body erect during exercise. Do not bend the knees to assist the upper-body muscles in the movement.

SEATED BEHIND-NECK PRESS

Starting Position: Take a seat on the bench with the feet flat on the floor. The head is up with the eyes facing straight ahead. The bar is behind the neck and across the shoulders and held with an overhand grip.

Action: Push the bar overhead until the arms are fully extended. Lower the bar to the starting position.

Precautions: Do not jerk the weight or use any unnecessary body motion during the movement.

STANDING DUMBBELL PRESS

Starting Position: Stand erect with the feet shoulder width apart. Grasp the dumbbells, and bring them to the shoulders with the palms facing forward.

Action: Push the dumbbell overhead until the arms are fully extended. Lower the dumbbells to the starting position.

Precautions: Do not jerk the dumbbells or bend the knees to assist in the movement. Keep the body erect during the motion.

SEATED DUMBBELL PRESS

Starting Position: Take a seat on the bench with the feet flat on the floor. Grasp the dumbbells, and bring them to the shoulders with the palms facing forward.

Action: Push the dumbbells overhead until the arms are fully extended. Lower the dumbbells to the starting position.

Precautions: Do not jerk the dumbbells or use any unnecessary body motion in the movement.

NOTE: This exercise can also be performed by alternating one arm then the other in the pressing movement.

LYING BARBELL TRICEPS EXTENSION

Starting Position: Lie flat on the bench with the feet flat on the floor. Grasp the bar with a narrow overhand grip so that the hands are about six inches or less apart. The arms are fully extended above the chest.

Action: Keep the upper arms extended, and lower the bar until it touches the forehead. Return to the starting position.

Precautions: Do not arch the body or allow the elbows to flare out to the sides during the movement.

STANDING BARBELL TRICEPS EXTENSION

Starting Position: Stand erect with the feet shoulder width apart. Grasp the bar with a narrow overhand grip so that the hands are about six inches or less apart. The arms are fully extended above the head.

Action: Keep the upper arms stationary, and lower the bar until it touches the back of the neck. Return to the starting position.

Precautions: Do not jerk the weight or bend the knees to assist in the lift. Do not allow the elbows to flare out to the sides during the movement.

Note: This exercise can also be performed in a seated position.

Lying Dumbbell Triceps Extension

Starting Position: Lie flat on the bench with the feet flat on the floor. Grasp the dumbbell in both hands with the fingers interlaced. The arms are fully extended above the chest.

Action: Keep the upper arms extended, and lower the dumbbell until it touches the back of the head. Return to the starting position.

Precautions: Do not arch the body or allow the elbows to flare out to the sides during the movement.

SEATED DUMBBELL TRICEPS EXTENSION

Starting Position: Take a seat on the bench with the feet flat on the floor. Grasp the dumbbell in both hands with the fingers interlaced. The arms are fully extended above the head.

Action: Keep the upper arms extended, and lower the dumbbell until it touches the back of the neck. Return to the starting position.

Precautions: Do not jerk the dumbbell or allow the elbows to flare out to the sides during the movement.

NOTE: Dumbbell triceps extensions can also be done in a standing position, or the exercise can be performed using a dumbbell held in one hand at a time.

DUMBBELL KICKBACK

Starting Position: Bend over at the waist until the upper torso is parallel to the floor. The feet are shoulder width apart. Grasp the dumbbells in both hands so that the palms are facing each other. The upper arms are parallel to the floor, and the forearms are bent at a 45° angle to the upper arms.

Action: Straighten both arms to the back until the elbows lock. Return to the starting position.

Precautions: Keep the body stationary, and do not jerk the dumbbells in the movement.

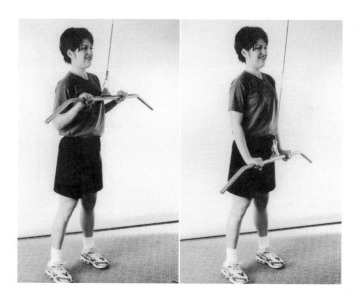

TRICEPS PRESS-DOWN

Starting Position: Stand erect with the feet shoulder width apart. Grasp the bar of the machine with a palms-down grip with the hands about six inches apart. The bar is chest height.

Action: Keep the upper arms stationary, and push the bar to the thighs by extending the forearms. Touch, and return to the starting position.

Precautions: Lean slightly in toward the bar while doing the exercise. Do not move the body to assist the triceps in extending the bar. Keep the elbows close to the body.

Wrist Curl

Starting Position: Take a seat on the bench with the feet flat on the floor. Grasp the bar with a palms-up grip, and support the arms on the thighs with the wrists extended beyond the knees. The wrists are relaxed so the bar is as low to the floor as possible.

Action: Curl the weight upward as high as possible without moving the forearms. Return to the starting position.

Precautions: Do not jerk the weight, and make sure that only the wrists move during the exercise.

REVERSE WRIST CURL

Starting Position: Take a seat on the bench with the feet flat on the floor. Grasp the bar with a palms-down grip, and support the arms on the thighs with the wrists extended beyond the knees. The wrists are relaxed so the bar is as low to the floor as possible.

Action: Curl the weight upward as high as possible without moving the forearms. Return to the starting position.

Precautions: Do not jerk the weight, and make sure that only the wrists move during the exercise.

DUMBBELL WRIST CURL

Starting Position: Take a seat on the bench with the feet flat on the floor. Grasp the dumbbell in each hand with a palms-up grip, and support the arms on the thighs with the wrists extended beyond the knees. The wrists are relaxed so the dumbbells are as low to the floor as possible.

Action: Curl the dumbbells upward as high as possible without moving the forearms. Return to the starting position.

Precautions: Do not jerk the weight, and make sure that only the wrists move during the exercise.

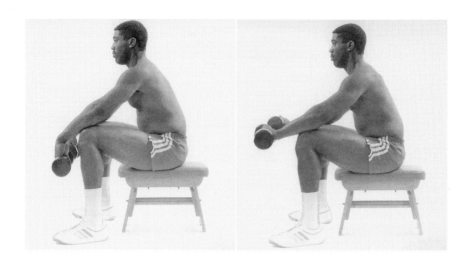

REVERSE DUMBBELL WRIST CURL

Starting Position: Take a seat on the bench with the feet flat on the floor. Grasp the dumbbell in each hand with a palms-down grip, and support the arms on the thighs with the wrists extended beyond the knees. The wrists are relaxed so the dumbbells are as low to the floor as possible.

Action: Curl the dumbbells upward as high as possible without moving the forearms. Return to the starting position.

Precautions: Do not jerk the weight, and make sure that only the wrists move during the exercise.

WRIST ROLLER

Starting Position: Stand erect with the feet about shoulder width apart. Grasp the bar with a palms-down grip with the hands approximately eight inches apart. The wrist roller consists of a weight attached to a bar by a three-foot length of rope. The arms are extended forward and parallel to the floor.

Action: Rotate the hands about the bar until all of the rope is wrapped around the bar. Return to the starting position.

Precautions: Do not move the body to assist in the movement, and do not allow the weight to drop on the extension because this could burn the hands.

NOTE: A clockwise rotation develops the wrist flexors, and a counter-clockwise rotation develops the wrist extensors.

SHOULDER

Upright Rowing

Starting Position: Stand erect with the feet about shoulder width apart. Grasp the bar with a palms-down grip with the hands about two inches apart. The arms are extended so the bar rests against the thighs.

Action: Keep the head up and the chest high. Raise the bar until it touches the chin. Return to the starting position.

Precautions: Do not move the body to assist in the exercise. Keep the bar close to the body with the elbows higher than the hands, and don't jerk to start the movement.

SIDE LATERAL RAISE

Starting Position: Stand erect with the feet about shoulder width apart. Grasp a dumbbell in each hand using an overhand grip. The arms are extended downward in front of the body.

Action: Raise the dumbbells upward to the sides of the body until the elbows lock and the arms are approximately parallel to the floor. Return to the starting position.

Precautions: Keep the body stationary, and do not jerk the dumbbells in the movement.

NOTE: You can vary the hand grip. As you change the palms from downward to upward, resistance is moved from the medial deltoid to the anterior deltoid.

Dips

Starting Position: The body is supported in a suspended position between the parallel bars with the arms fully extended.

Action: Dip downward as far as possible. Return to the starting position.

Precautions: Avoid unnecessary body swing in the movement. Add weights to the body to increase the resistance, if needed.

NOTE: If it is not possible to do the dip as described, the resistance can be decreased as shown in the following pictures.

Seated Dips

Starting Position: The body is supported on two benches by placing the feet on one bench and the hands on the other. The arms are fully extended, and the back is straight.

Action: Bend the arms, and allow the body to lower as far as possible. Return to the starting position.

Precautions: Avoid unnecessary body movement in performing the exercise. Weights can be placed on the upper thighs to increase the resistance, if needed.

CHEST

BARBELL BENCH PRESS

Starting Position: Lie flat on the bench with the knees bent and feet flat on the floor. Use a palms-up grip, approximately the width of the shoulders. Hold the bar in a chest-rest position.

Action: Press the bar directly upward until elbows lock, and then return to the starting position.

Precautions: Do not arch the back or raise the buttocks during movement. Do not bounce the weight off the chest.

NOTE: This exercise can be done using a narrow grip to increase resistance to the triceps.

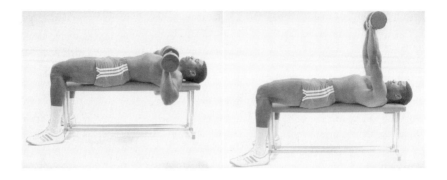

DUMBBELL BENCH PRESS

Starting Position: Lie flat on the bench with the knees bent and feet flat on the floor. Grasp the dumbbells with a palms-up grip. Hold the dumbbells in a chest-rest position.

Action: Press the dumbbells directly upward until elbows lock, and return to the starting position.

Precautions: Do not arch the back or raise the buttocks during movement. Keep the elbows away from the body and pointed outward.

Barbell Incline Bench Press

Starting Position: Lie flat on inclined bench with legs straight and feet flat against supports. Use a palms-up grip, approximately the width of the shoulders. Hold the bar in a chest-rest position.

Action: Press the bar upward until elbows lock, and then return to the starting position.

Precautions: Do not arch the back or raise the buttocks during movement. Do not bounce weight off the chest.

Dumbbell Incline Bench Press

Starting Position: Lie flat on inclined bench with legs straight and feet flat against the floor. Grasp the dumbbells with a palms-up grip, and hold them in a chest-rest position.

Action: Press the dumbbells upward until the elbows lock, and then return to the starting position.

Precautions: Do not arch the back or raise the buttocks during the movement. Keep the elbows away from the body and pointed outward.

BENCH FLYS

Starting Position: Lie flat on bench. Hold dumbbell in each hand, straight up over the chest with the palms inward.

Action: Lower the dumbbells with the arms straight until the arms are parallel to the floor, and then return to the starting position.

Precautions: Do not arch the back or raise the buttocks. Lower and raise the dumbbells slowly.

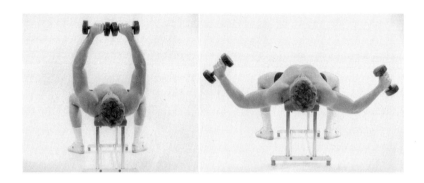

BENT-ARM FLYS

Starting Position: Lie flat on bench. Hold a dumbbell in each hand with the arms extended over the chest in a semiflexed position.

Action: Lower the dumbbells with the arms semiflexed, as far as they can go toward the floor. Return to the starting position.

Precautions: Keep the arms semiflexed. Do not arch the back or raise the buttocks. Lower and raise the dumbbells slowly.

Decline Press

Starting Position: Lie back on a 30° decline bench with the head at the lower end and the knees hooked over the top of bench. Use a palms-up grip approximately the width of the shoulder. Hold the bar in a chest-rest position.

Action: Press the bar upward at approximately 60° until elbows lock, and then return to the starting position.

Precautions: Do not arch the back or raise the buttocks during movement. Do not bounce the weight off the chest.

BENT-ARM PULLOVER

Starting Position: Lie flat on bench with knees bent and feet flat on the floor. Allow head to hang over the end of the bench. Use a palms-up grip with the hands approximately twelve inches apart. Hold the bar in a chest-rest position.

Action: Lower the bar back overhead as far as possible with the elbows bent. Pull the weight back to the starting position.

Precautions: Keep elbows close to the head and pointing toward the ceiling during the exercise. Avoid unnecessary arching of back. Do not jerk or make unnecessary body movements. Keep the bar close to face during the exercise movement.

Pull-Up

Starting Position: Use a palms-down grip, approximately the width of the shoulders, with arms extended to support body suspended from the bar.

Action: Pull body upward to the bar until the chin is above the bar, and then return to the starting position.

Precautions: Straighten out arms on each repetition. Avoid unnecessary body swing and movement. Add weights to body to increase the resistance, if needed.

NOTE: If you cannot do the pull-up as described, it is possible to decrease the resistance as shown in the second set of pictures.

LAT PULL-DOWN

Starting Position: Start in a seated position. Grasp bar in a wide palms-down grip with arms fully extended.

Action: Pull the bar down until it touches the base of the neck, and then return to the starting position.

Precautions: Keep the upper body straight. Do not jerk or raise body to assist in the movement.

NOTE: The same exercise can be done but with the bar pulled downward in front of the chest.

BENT-OVER ROWING

Starting Position: Start in a bent-over position with the upper torso parallel to the floor. The feet are shoulder width apart with the knees slightly bent. Grasp the bar with an overhand grip with the arms fully extended.

Action: Pull the bar upward until it touches the rib cage, and then return to the starting position.

Precautions: Keep the spine in an arched position to take pressure off the lower back. Do not jerk the weight or raise the body to assist in the movement.

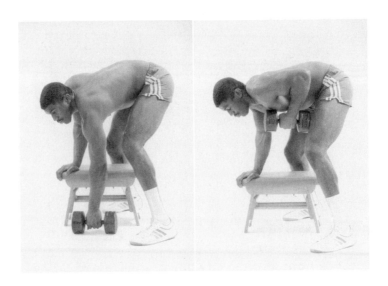

DUMBBELL BENT-OVER ROWING

Starting Position: Start in a bent-over position with the upper torso parallel to the floor. The feet are shoulder width apart with the knees slightly bent. Grasp the dumbbell with the arm fully extended, the opposite arm supporting the body by contacting a bench for stability.

Action: Pull the dumbbell upward until it touches the torso, and then return to the starting position.

Precautions: Keep the elbow close to the body while doing the exercise. Do not jerk the weight or raise the body to assist in the movement.

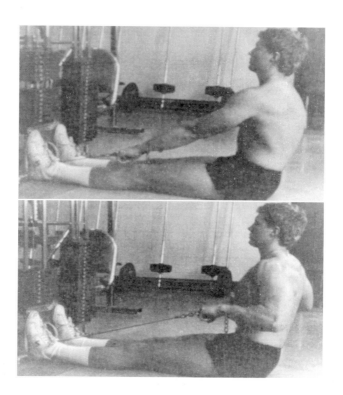

SEATED ROWING

Starting Position: Take a seated position with the legs fully extended and braced against the machine. Grasp the bar with a palms-down grip and the arms extended.

Action: Pull the bar toward the body until it touches the lower chest, and then return to the starting position.

Precautions: Keep the back straight during the exercise. Do not jerk to assist in the movement.

NOTE: This exercise can be done with a palms-up grip, which will utilize the biceps of the arm to a greater amount.

Dead Lift

Starting Position: Stand next to the bar with the front of legs touching the bar and the feet shoulder width apart. Bend down and grasp the bar with the palms facing toward the legs and the hands about shoulder width apart. Bend the legs with the hips lowered and head up. Arch the back to take stress off the lower back.

Action: Pull the bar up along the legs until the body is upright and the bar is on the front of the thighs. Then return to the starting position.

Precautions: Keep the bar close to the legs to reduce back strain. Always keep the head up and lift with the legs.

GOOD MORNING

Starting Position: Stand with the bar behind the neck and resting on the shoulders. The feet are shoulder width apart with the legs straight.

Action: Bend forward at the waist until the upper torso is parallel with the floor, and then return to the starting position.

Precautions: Since this exercise puts stress on the lower back muscles, it is important to start with light resistance at first. Keep the head up at all times, and do not jerk to assist in the movement.

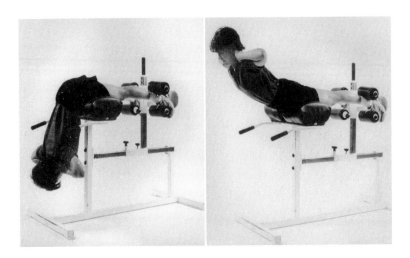

BACK RAISE

Starting Position: Take a prone position on the machine with the lower part of the body on the machine and the upper torso bent forward over the machine. The hands are interlocked behind the neck. It may be necessary to have a partner support the lower body by pushing down on the legs.

Action: Raise the upper torso upward until the body is parallel to the floor, and then return to the starting position.

Precautions: Do not hyperextend the back by going above parallel. Do not jerk or use any unnecessary motion to assist in the movement.

SHRUGS

Starting Position: Stand upright and grasp the bar with a palms-down grip with the arms fully extended.

Action: Elevate the shoulder girdle as high as possible, and then return to the starting position.

Precautions: Keep the body straight, and do not bend the arms when raising the weight.

Bent-Over Lateral Raise

Starting Position: Start in a bent-over position with the upper torso parallel to the floor. The feet are shoulder width apart with the knees slightly bent. Grasp the dumbbells in each hand with the arms fully extended.

Action: Raise the dumbbells lateral from the body until the arms are parallel to the floor, and then return to the starting position.

Precautions: Keep the head up, and do not jerk the weight or raise the body to assist in the movement.

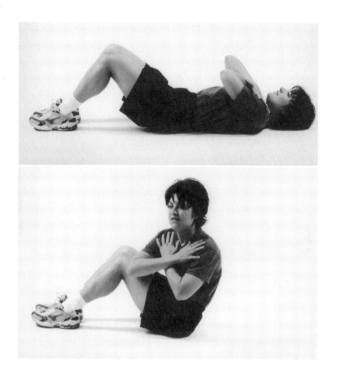

CURL-UP

Starting Position: Lie flat on the floor with legs bent at the knees and the feet flat on the floor. The hands are folded over the chest.

Action: Curl up to approximately a 30° angle. Rotate the right side of body toward left knee, and return to the starting position. On the next repetition rotate body toward right knee.

Precautions: Do not stabilize the feet unless absolutely necessary. Do not arch the back during the exercise, and keep the arms flat against the chest. Be sure to start by bending the head forward and progressively curl up to the 30° angle. Curl back to the starting position by touching lower back, upper back, and finally the head. A good check is to have someone place a hand under the lower back; the body should press down on the hand until the lower back is curled forward.

NOTE: If the curl-up cannot be done as described, it is possible to decrease the resistance by placing the hands alongside the hips instead of over the chest. To increase the resistance, weights can be held on the chest while doing the exercise. Another method is to use an incline board and raise the board to provide a greater amount of resistance.

V-Sit

Starting Position: Lie flat on the floor with the legs straight and the arms fully extended above the head.

Action: Raise the legs and arms at the same time, and touch the hands and feet together above the body. Hold this position for one second and return to the starting position.

Precautions: Keep the arms and legs straight while doing the exercise. Do not jerk or make any unnecessary motion to assist in the movement.

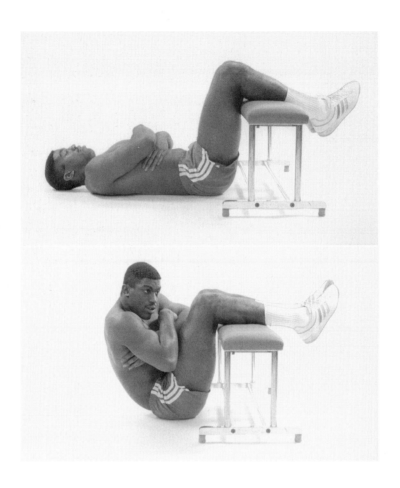

Roman Chair Curl-Up

Starting Position: Lie flat on the floor with knees bent over a bench. The hands are folded over the chest. To increase resistance, weights can be held on the chest.

Action: Curl up and rotate the body until right side of body touches left knee and return to the starting position. On next repetition rotate body to the right knee.

Precautions: Do not arch back during the curl-up. Do not jerk the body during the movement.

Hanging Knee-Up

Starting Position: Grasp the bar and allow the body to be completely extended.

Action: Raise the legs, knees bent, until the knees touch the chest, and return to the starting position.

Precautions: Raise the legs slowly without jerking to assist in the movement.

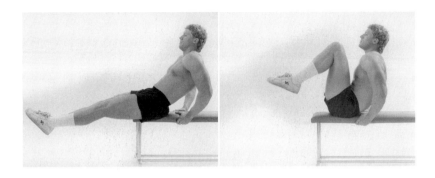

SITTING KNEE-UP

Starting Position: Sit on the end of the bench with the legs extended away from the bench. Lean the upper torso back and grasp the bench with the hands.

Action: Slowly bend your knees and raise them to the chest. Touch the knees against the chest, and return to the starting position.

Precautions: Hold the feet and knees together during the exercise. Do not jerk the body during the movement.

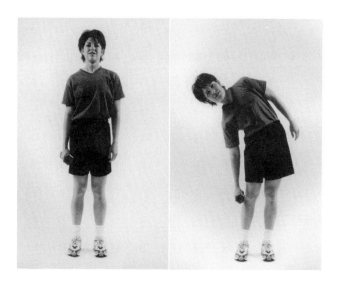

Side Bend

Starting Position: Stand upright with a dumbbell held in one hand and the arms completely extended.

Action: Bend sideways as far as possible toward the side with the dumbbell and return to the starting position. When the desired number of repetitions have been completed, change the dumbbell to the other hand and repeat the exercise to the other side.

Precautions: Do not jerk the weight or use any unnecessary motion in the movement.

TWISTS

Starting Position: Take a straddle seated position on a bench with the back straight and the head looking forward. Place the bar behind the neck and across the shoulders.

Action: Keep the pelvic region locked and twist the upper torso as far as possible to the right. Return to the starting position, and then twist to the left and return to the starting position.

Precautions: Squeeze with the knees against the bench to keep the hips from rotating. Do not jerk the body during the movement.

LEG

LEG SPLITS

Starting Position: Lie flat on the right side of the body with the right hand and arm under the head. Use the left arm to support the body in the proper position during the exercise.

Action: Raise the left leg as high as possible and return to the starting position. When the desired number of repetitions have been completed on the right side, change to the left side and repeat the exercise.

Precautions: Keep the leg straight at all times, and do not jerk the body in the movement.

NOTE: To increase the resistance, weights can be added to the feet and ankles.

SQUAT

Starting Position: Stand erect with the feet about shoulder width apart. The toes are pointed slightly out. Place the bar behind the neck and across the shoulders. Keep the head up and the back straight.

Action: Spread the chest and lock the lower back. The downward movement is started by bending at the hips and sticking out the gluteal area. (Think of sitting in a chair.) Lower the body until the thighs are parallel with the floor. Return to the starting position.

Precautions: Have partners assist as spotters during the exercise. Keep back straight and chest high throughout the movement. Rounding the back can place stress on spine and cause injury. Do not bounce at the bottom of the squat. As a safety device, place a bench behind the lifter, which will allow the lifter to sit down if balance is lost.

NOTE: This exercise can be performed to any selected joint angle of the legs depending on the needs of the person training.

FRONT SQUAT

Starting Position: Stand erect with the feet about shoulder width apart. The toes are pointed slightly out. Hold the bar in front of the neck and across the shoulders. Support the bar by wrapping the hands around the bar with an overhead grip. Keep the head up and the back straight.

Action: The downward movement is started by bending at the hips and sticking out the gluteal area. (Think of sitting in a chair.) Lower the body until the thighs are parallel to the floor. Return to the starting position.

Precautions: Keep the upper torso straight to remove stress from the lower back. Do not bounce at the bottom of the squat.

NOTE: This exercise can be performed to any selected joint angle of the legs depending on the needs of the person training.

Hack Squat

Starting Position: Stand erect with the feet about shoulder width apart. The bar is placed behind the back and against the thighs. Grasp the bar with an overhand grip, and keep the head up and the back straight.

Action: Lower the body until the thighs are parallel with the floor. Return to the starting position.

Precautions: Keep the upper torso straight to remove stress from the lower back. Do not bounce at the bottom of the squat.

Note: This exercise can be performed at any selected joint angle depending on the needs of the person training.

LUNGE SQUAT

Starting Position: Stand erect with the feet about shoulder width apart. Place the bar behind the neck and across the shoulders. Keep the head up and the back straight.

Action: Step forward with the right leg and lower the body until the left knee is about twelve inches from the floor. Return to the starting position. Repeat the same action with the left leg, and return to the starting position.

Precautions: Keep the back straight and the head up during the movement. Do not bounce at the bottom part of the exercise.

Trap Bar

The trap bar is an excellent lead-up exercise to squats. It is a safe exercise, as you do not need a spotter. You can also combine shoulder shrugs with this exercise.

Starting Position: Stand with the feet about shoulder width apart. The toes are pointed slightly out. Lower the body by bending at the hips and extending the gluteal area. (Think of sitting in a chair.) Grasp the hand grips on the bar, which will allow the weight to be in perfect alignment with the body's center of gravity. Keep the head up.

Action: Spread the chest and lock the lower back, then extend the legs until you are in a standing position. Then return to the starting position.

Precautions: Keep the upper torso straight to remove stress from the lower back. Rounding the back can cause stress and injury.

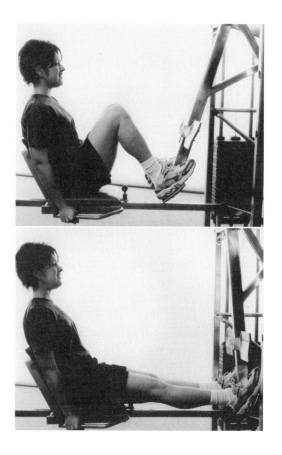

LEG PRESS

Starting Position: Take a seat in the machine, and grasp the handles on both sides of the seat with the feet on the pedals. Keep the back straight.

Action: Push forward until the legs are fully extended. Return to the starting position.

Precautions: Do not use any unnecessary body motion to aid in the movement.

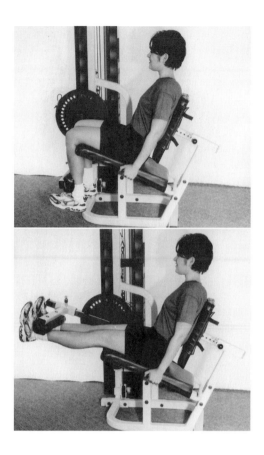

LEG EXTENSION

Starting Position: Sit on the edge of the seat and place your feet behind the pads of the machine. Support the body by grasping the sides of the bench. Keep the back straight.

Action: Fully extend the legs to a locked position. Return to the starting position.

Precautions: Do not jerk the weight or use any unnecessary body motion in the movement.

NOTE: It is possible to isolate the leg muscles by doing single leg extensions.

DUMBBELL JUMP SQUAT

Starting Position: Assume a front-back foot position, and hold the dumbbells with the arms fully extended. Squat down to about a 90° position.

Action: Jump upward as high as possible. Prior to returning to the starting position, switch the feet and flex the knees to absorb the downward force.

Precautions: Make sure to flex the ankles, knees, and hips when landing to reduce the downward shock.

BENCH JUMP

Starting Position: Stand erect with the body sideways to the bench.

Action: Flex the knees and jump sideways over the bench. Touch this side and return to the starting side.

Precautions: Use the arms to aid in the jump to increase height. Make sure to flex the ankles, knees, and hips when landing to reduce the downward shock.

STANDING HEEL RAISE

Starting Position: Stand erect with the feet about eight inches apart. Place the bar behind the neck and across the shoulders. Keep the head up and the back straight. Put the balls of the feet on a four-inch wooden board, and allow the heels to lower as far as possible.

Action: Raise the body as high as possible. Return to the starting position.

Precautions: Keep the body erect, and do the exercise slowly to maintain balance.

SINGLE-HEEL RAISE

Starting Position: Place the right foot on a four-inch board, and allow the heel to lower as far as possible. Hold a dumbbell in the right hand with the arm extended. Keep the body erect and balanced by holding on to a support with the left hand.

Action: Raise the body as high as possible. Return to the starting position. When the repetitions for the right leg have been completed, switch to the left leg.

Precautions: Keep the body erect, and do the exercise slowly to maintain balance.

Sitting Heel Raise

Starting Position: Take a seated position on the bench. Place the bar across the top of the thigh and support the weight with the hands. Place the balls of the feet on a four-inch wooden board, and allow the heels to lower as far as possible.

Action: Raise the heels as high as possible. Return to the starting position.

Precautions: Keep the body erect, and do not bounce at the bottom of the movement.

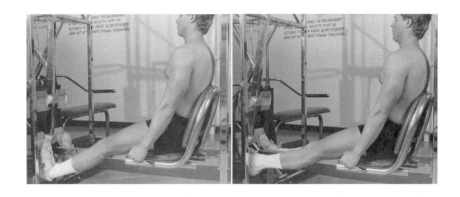

Toe Extension

Starting Position: Take a seat in the machine, and fully extend the legs. Grasp the handles on both sides of the seat, and keep the back straight. Slide the feet off the pedals until only the balls of the feet make contact.

Action: Extend the toes as far forward as possible. Return to the starting position.

Precautions: Keep the legs straight, and do the exercise slowly.

NOTE: To change the calf development, it is possible to use different toe placements on the pedals as shown in the pictures.

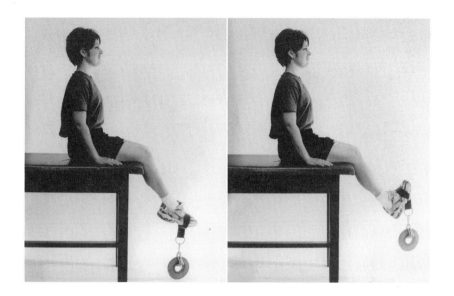

TOE RAISE

Starting Position: Sit on the edge of a table with the lower legs hanging over the side. Grasp the side of the table with the hands to maintain balance. Attach a weight to the toes of the foot with a strap or rope.

Action: Lift the toes upward toward the shins as far as possible. Return to the starting position.

Precautions: Isolate the movement of the front part of the foot, and do the exercise slowly.

NOTE: This exercise can also be performed using one foot at a time.

Donkey Raise

Starting Position: Bend over a bench from the waist until the upper torso is parallel to the floor. Support your body with the hands on the bench. Place the balls of the feet on a four-inch wooden board, and allow the heels to lower as far as possible. Have a partner sit astride the hips to provide resistance.

Action: Raise the body as high as possible. Return to the starting position.

Precautions: Do not use any unnecessary motion in the movement. Have the partner sit back as far as possible because this will provide more resistance in the exercise.

Front Leg Kick

Starting Position: Stand erect with the right leg attached to pulley from the machine. Maintain balance by holding on to a support. The right foot is approximately sixteen inches behind the left foot.

Action: Extend the right leg forward and as high as possible. Return to the starting position. When the repetitions for the right leg have been completed, switch to the left leg.

Precautions: Keep the leg straight at all times, and do not bend the knee. Do the exercise slowly to maintain balance.

SIDE LEG KICK

Starting Position: Stand erect and sideways to the machine with the right leg attached to the pulley. Maintain balance by holding on to a support. The right leg is crossed over the left leg away from the machine as far as possible.

Action: Extend the right leg outward as far as possible. Return to the starting position. When the repetitions for the right leg have been completed, switch to the left.

Precautions: Keep the leg straight at all times, and do not bend the knee. Do the exercise slowly to maintain balance.

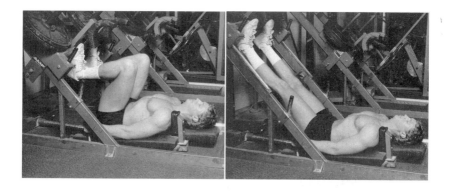

Vertical Leg Press

Starting Position: Lie flat on the back with the legs bent and the feet against the bar. The hips should be directly beneath the feet.

Action: Push the bar upward until the legs are fully extended. Return to the starting position.

Precautions: Since the resistance on this exercise has a tendency to cause the pressure in the chest cavity to increase, the lifter should keep the mouth open during the movement.

Note: This exercise can be modified so that the calf muscles can be trained by extending the front of the foot while the legs are extended.

Leg Curl

Starting Position: Lie face downward on the bench with the legs extended and the backs of the feet against the pads. Grasp the sides of the bench to maintain balance.

Action: Lift the feet upward until the pads touch the buttocks. Return to the starting position.

Precautions: Movement should be entirely in the knee joint. Avoid unnecessary jerking or body movement.

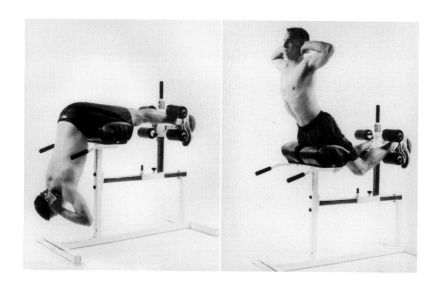

GLUTE-HAM RAISE

Starting Position: Take a prone position on the machine with the lower part of the body on the machine and the upper torso bent forward to form a 90° angle. The hands are interlocked behind the neck.

Action: Raise the upper torso upward until the body is parallel to the floor. Start to bend the knees and continue to raise the upper torso until it is also perpendicular to the floor. Hold this position for one count, and then return to the starting position.

Precautions: Do not jerk or use any unnecessary motion to assist in the movement. There should not be any undue stress on the lower back while doing this exercise.

POWER CLEAN

Starting Position: Place the feet about shoulder width apart, and allow the shins to touch the bar. Bend down and grasp the bar with an overhand grip with the hands about shoulder width on the bar. Bend the knees until the hips are slightly lower than the knees. Keep the head up and the arms fully extended.

Action: Straighten the legs to lift the weight. Keep the arms extended. Push forward with the hips as the legs extend upward. As the body starts to become erect, pull upward with the arms fully extended. As the bar

reaches maximum height, drop the body under the bar by flexing the hips and knees into a squat position and catch the weight by moving the elbows under the bar and support the bar across the chest at the base of the neck. Stand up by extending the hips and knees to a fully erect position. To return to the starting position lower the bar in a controlled fashion by keeping the arms fully extended and squat with the legs until the weight touches the floor.

Precautions: Be sure you use an explosive movement in this exercise. Start with a light weight and practice the technique before using heavy weights.

Strength Training for Athletes

CHAPTER 6

Anyone who wishes to improve athletic performance can do so by utilizing strength training. As indicated in chapter 1, to increase power, the rate of doing work, one must increase either strength or velocity or, if possible, both of these factors. Since all athletic contests are time related, a person who can increase work output for a given time frame will be more successful.

Research indicates a high correlation between strength levels and velocity. Weight training was once thought to reduce flexibility or cause a person to be muscle-bound and slow. The research refutes this myth and indicates instead that by using weight training through a full range of motion, athletes actually improve their flexibility and speed of movement.

The advantage of increased strength is important to both male and female athletes. Both can engage in a strength development program to increase their efficiency. At the end of this chapter, an athlete or coach can devise an individualized strength training program for any sport.

STRESS AND OVERTRAINING

Some years ago Hans Selye, a medical doctor, discovered that all stressors that the human body encounters produce very similar biochemical responses. He found that stressors cause the body to go through stages, which Selye termed the general adaptation syndrome (GAS). The stages are as follows:

1. Alarm reaction—This is the initial response to the stressor and causes a mobilization of the body systems to withstand the stressor. This up-

sets homeostasis, or the body's equilibrium. An example is the stress involved in starting a strength program.

2. Stage of resistance—During this stage the body improves its capacity and builds up reserves to combat the stressors. This stage represents the objective of a physical conditioning program. As a result of this stage in a strength training program, the body increases its ability to exert force and has a greater work output.

3. Stage of exhaustion (overtraining)—This stage is brought about by the body's inability to withstand chronic stress. It can result in exhaustion caused by overtraining; in the sport world, it is sometimes referred to as athletic staleness. Some of the symptoms of this stage are as follows:

❐ increased resting heart rate
❐ increased exercise heart rate
❐ decreased appetite
❐ decreased body weight
❐ sleep loss
❐ decreased sex drive
❐ generalized body aches and pains
❐ increased release of catecholamines (hormones) from the adrenal gland
❐ decreased sports efficiency, loss of concentration, and errors in judgment
❐ interpersonal problems and conflicts
❐ illness and injury

When planning a training program, one must take into consideration the total stressor influence that is going to act upon the athlete. Such things as training loads, family influence, workload at school, social interactions, and employment are important. Always remember that too much stress leads to overtraining and the stage of exhaustion.

PERIODIZATION

To prevent overtraining and bring about peak performance in strength development, a system of training known as periodization has been recommended. Periodization is a training approach that involves dividing the training year into major phases or cycles, during which the stress of training is manipulated by varying the volume and intensity of the training stimulus during the selected phases. This combats overtraining and the on-set of the stage of exhaustion (athletic staleness).

Volume is the amount of training completed in a given training or workout period. In strength training it represents all the sets and repetitions and can be quantified as the total number of pounds lifted. *Intensity* is the difficulty of the training stimulus. In strength training it is determined by the percentage of a one-repetition maximum (1 RM).

The periodization model for strength training (see Table 6.1) is divided into five yearly phases: hypertrophy, basic strength, strength and power, peaking or maintenance, and active rest.

In each phase in Table 6.1, the suggested volume and intensity are given. These factors are controlled by the number of sets and maximum repetitions performed during the workout. Ranges in both sets and repetitions allow variation in the stress of the selected workout for each period. The number of training days per week are also provided.

For example, if an athlete is in the hypertrophy phase, he or she would do three to ten sets of 8 to 12 RM for three to four days per week. This type of program would have a low intensity and a high volume. By following such a plan, the athlete would be better prepared to avoid the risk of overtraining.

Table 6.1 Periodization Model For Strength Training

Phase	Hyper-trophy	Basic Strength	Strength and Power	Peaking or Maintenance	Active Rest
Sets	3–10	3–5	3–5	1–3	
Repetitions (RM)	8–12	4–6	2–3	1–3	
Days/Week	3–4	3–5	3–5	1–5	
Intensity	low	high	high	very high to low	
Volume	high	moderate to high	low	very low	

Source: Adapted from Michael Stone and Harold O'Bryant, *Weight Training: A Scientific Approach*, (Edina, Minn.: Burgess International Group, *1987*), *123*. Reprinted by permission of the publisher.
Sets do not include warm-up sets.

Periodization Phases

Hypertrophy Phase: In this phase the goal is to stimulate the tissues that make up the joint-lever system and bring about an increase in the mass of the tissue. The focus is on increasing the size of the muscle cells; thus the term *hypertrophy* is used. During this phase the volume (number of exercises, sets, and repetitions) will be high, and the intensity (percentage of 1 RM) will be relatively low.

Basic Strength Phase: During this phase the intensity will be relatively high, and the volume will be moderate to high. The goal is to stimulate the increased lean body mass obtained in the hypertrophy phase and make it as strong as possible.

Strength and Power Phase: After completing the basic strength phase, the goal is to continue to increase strength, but also increase the power output. This phase focuses not only on stimulating the tissues that produce a force, but also on stimulating the systems that provide the energy to allow the body to move very rapidly. In many sports the first three steps are the most critical in achieving success. During this phase the intensity is high and the volume is low.

Peaking or Maintenance Phase: This is the phase when the athlete is competing and more time must be used to increase skill and prepare for games. Maintaining the strength training effects is important, and thus a strength training program is a critical part of this phase. During this time the volume is low and, depending on the day of the week, the intensity may be either very high or very low.

Active Rest: This phase follows completion of the competition phase and refers to participating in some other activity or the same activity at very low volumes and intensities. The length of active rest depends on the sport and the athlete's needs. This phase allows the athlete to combat overtraining, which leads to decreased performance.

Factors in Setting Up a Periodization Plan

When setting up a periodization plan, the following factors should be considered:

1. What are the demands of the sport? How can these best be developed? What is the athlete trying to develop at this time of the training year?

What facilities are available for training? How much time is available for training?

2. What are the demands of the position? Is it a wide receiver, a power forward, or a center-blocker in volleyball?

3. Determine the athlete's strengths and weaknesses. What is the basic training background of the athlete? Should the athlete engage in a beginning strength program to develop overall strength before starting a periodized training plan?

In addition to considering the previous factors in writing strength training programs for athletes, one must also understand the concept of using core and supplementary exercises to bring about the desired changes to increase performance.

CORE AND SUPPLEMENTARY EXERCISES

A core exercise is a strength exercise that uses a large muscle mass and is usually a multiple-joint exercise. Examples of core exercises are the bench press, incline press, squats, leg press, and power clean. Core exercises form the foundation of the strength training program and contribute to total body strength.

Supplementary exercises utilize a smaller muscle mass. Many times they are single-joint exercises that increase the strength of the specific muscles used in a given activity.

Table 6.2 contains a list of various sports and strength training exercises that could be considered to increase the strength of the muscles used in the sport. An athlete can now select one or more exercises for each specific body part.

Table 6.2 Weight Training Exercises for Specific Sports

	Arm curl	Back raise	Bench flys	Bench jump	Bench press	Bent-arm pullover	Bent-over lateral raise	Bent-over rowing	Curl-up	Dead lift	Dip	Dumbbell bent-over rowing	Dumbbell curl	Heel raise
Archery	✓		✓		✓		✓	✓	✓				✓	
Badminton			✓		✓	✓			✓					
Baseball					✓			✓	✓			✓	✓	
Basketball	✓			✓	✓				✓	✓				✓
Bicycling					✓				✓	✓				
Bowling	✓				✓				✓					✓
Boxing	✓				✓			✓	✓		✓			
Canoeing	✓				✓	✓	✓	✓	✓					
Climbing	✓				✓		✓		✓		✓			
Crew	✓	✓			✓			✓	✓			✓		
Diving					✓				✓	✓				
Fencing					✓				✓		✓			
Field hockey	✓				✓				✓					✓
Football	✓				✓	✓			✓	✓			✓	
Golf	✓				✓	✓			✓					
Handball		✓			✓				✓					✓
Hockey	✓				✓			✓			✓			✓
Martial arts	✓	✓			✓	✓			✓					✓

Incline bench press	Lat pull-down	Leg curl	Leg extension	Leg press	Neck exercise	Overhead press	Power clean	Sitting heel raise	Seated rowing	Side lateral raise	Single-heel raise	Squat	Toe extension	Triceps extension	Upright rowing	Wrist curl
	■	■		■									■			■
	■	■										■	■		■	
	■		■									■	■	■	■	■
	■		■							■		■		■	■	■
	■		■									■		■	■	■
	■					■				■		■		■	■	
■	■									■		■		■		■
	■					■				■		■		■		■
■	■					■				■		■	■	■	■	■
■	■					■						■		■		
■	■					■						■	■	■		■
■	■					■				■		■		■		■
■	■					■			■			■			■	■
■	■		■			■		■				■	■			■
	■		■							■		■		■	■	■
	■											■		■	■	■
■	■									■	■					■
		■			■					■	■	■	■	■	■	■

Continued.

Table 6.2 Continued

	Arm curl	Back raise	Bench flys	Bench jump	Bench press	Bent-arm pullover	Bent-over lateral raise	Bent-over rowing	Curl-up	Dead lift	Dip	Dumbbell bent-over rowing	Dumbbell curl	Heel raise
Racquetball		X		X			X		X		X			
Rugby	X	X			X				X				X	
Skating									X					
Skiing	X								X				X	
Soccer				X		X								
Softball	X		X			X			X			X		
Squash		X			X			X				X		
Swimming		X			X	X			X			X		
Tennis	X	X	X						X				X	
Track—distance					X				X	X				
Track—sprints			X						X			X		
Field events			X		X							X		
Volleyball		X			X	X			X				X	
Water Polo	X				X			X						
Wrestling	X	X			X				X		X			

Incline bench press	Lat pull-down	Leg curl	Leg extension	Leg press	Neck exercise	Overhead press	Power clean	Sitting heel raise	Seated rowing	Side lateral raise	Single-heel raise	Squat	Toe extension	Triceps extension	Upright rowing	Wrist curl
	■	■	■					■				■	■	■	■	
■	■	■	■	■	■	■			■			■	■	■		
	■									■		■	■			
	■		■									■	■		■	
	■		■			■						■	■	■	■	■
	■									■		■	■	■	■	■
	■		■						■			■	■	■	■	■
	■					■				■		■	■	■	■	■
	■	■										■	■	■	■	■
	■		■									■	■	■	■	■
■	■						■					■	■	■	■	■
	■		■					■		■		■	■	■	■	
	■	■	■						■			■	■		■	
	■	■		■	■							■	■		■	■

OFF-SEASON STRENGTH TRAINING PROGRAM

Here is an example of how the information in tables 6.1 and 6.2 can be used to write an off-season strength program for a football defensive lineman who is in the hypertrophy phase of the training year. Using this program will increase the amount of lean body mass (hypertrophy) and also increase strength.

Sport: football   **Position:** defensive lineman

Period: hypertrophy

Core Exercises: bench press, squats, power clean

Supplementary Exercises: partner resistance, arm curl, dumbbell triceps extension, upright rowing, lat pull-down, Roman chair curl-up, leg curl

Warm-up: Start each exercise with a warm-up set using a resistance that is approximately 50 percent of your 1 RM for eight to ten repetitions.

Note: In each workout set the last repetition should be a maximum effort.

 Off-Season Strength Training Program

Body Parts	Exercise	Sets	Reps (RM)	Recovery
1. Neck	Partner resistance	3	10	2 min.
2. Arms				
a. Biceps	Arm curl	4	10	2 min.
b. Triceps	Dumbbell triceps extension	4	10	2 min.
c. Shoulders	Upright rowing	4	10	2 min.
3. Chest	Bench Press	4	10	2 min.
4. Back	Lat pull-down	4	10	2 min.
5. Midsection	Roman chair curl-up	3	30	3 min.
6. Legs	Squats	4	10	2 min.
	Leg curl	4	10	2 min.
7. Total Body	Power clean	4	5	2 min.

Modified Periodization Program

Many athletes, especially at the high school level, participate in more than one sport and cannot follow a full year of periodized training such as that of a single-sport athlete. Some athletes may play football, then basketball, and then baseball. They still want to obtain the benefits of a good strength program so that they can continue to increase their power output and obtain optimal performance levels.

Using a modified periodization program has been highly successful in bringing about beneficial results. This program is a combination of core and supplementary exercises. The core exercises have both a five-set day and a three-set day for each exercise.

Five-Set Day
1. Warm-up
2. Three sets at 80 percent of a 1 RM for four repetitions
3. Two sets at 90 percent of a 1 RM for two repetitions

Three-Set Day
1. Warm-up
2. Two sets at 80 percent of a 1 RM for four repetitions
3. One set at 90 percent of a 1 RM for two repetitions

Supplementary Exercises: Generally do two sets of 10 RM. In the off-season usually do no more than five different exercises, and in-season usually do two or three different exercises.

The following is an example of a training program for a three-sport athlete:

Core Exercises
1. Squat
2. Power clean
3. Bench press

Supplementary Exercises

Off-season = five exercises determined by the athlete's strength training goals.

In-season = two to three exercises selected in the sport in which the athlete is currently participating.

NEBRASKA ATHLETIC TEST

The major reason an athlete engages in a strength training program is to increase power output. As stated earlier, power output determines how much work can be accomplished in a given amount of time.

The University of Nebraska has one of the most outstanding programs in the world to condition athletes. The program uses four tests that seem to predict athletic performance. These tests can be utilized to determine if the strength training program is making positive changes that will aid the athlete. The four tests are the ten-yard dash, the forty-yard dash, the twenty-yard shuttle run, and the vertical jump.

All that is needed to administer the tests are a stopwatch, a wall with a measuring board marked in one-half-inch increments, and a gym floor or grassy area. A worksheet for this test can be found in Appendix G.

THE SPORT EXPERIENCE

Write an individualized strength training program for your selected sport and record your work on the sports training worksheet in Appendix E or the modified periodization worksheet in Appendix F. In addition, take the Nebraska Athletic Test as explained on the worksheet in Appendix G to determine how well you perform before starting your strength program.

Bodybuilding and Physique Training

CHAPTER **7**

Bodybuilder is defined as a person who uses strength training to obtain a more muscular physique. This broad definition includes nearly all people who lift weights. As indicated earlier, the majority of men and women who enroll in beginning weight training classes desire to "look better"; in other words, they wish to be "bodybuilders."

The training programs described previously can help develop the different muscles of the body and bring about a more muscular physique.

PHYSIQUE ATHLETES

Another group of individuals who have a great desire to affect the muscular system of the body are classified as physique athletes. The elite athletes in this group earn Mr. America, Mr. Universe, and Mr. Olympia titles. This group also includes females who compete for similar titles such as Miss America and Miss Universe.

Most physique contests are judged according to the following criteria:

1. *Symmetry:* the overall balance of development of the various body parts and muscle groups
2. *Muscularity:* how well a muscle is developed in regard to size, definition, and hardness
3. *Presentation:* personal grooming, posing ability, and how individuals project themselves

Even when using a mirror, it is impossible for people to see themselves as they really are. Many times we view ourselves quite differently from what is reflected. To record changes and understand more about your body, you should measure the various body parts at the start of a training program and take periodic measurements to determine how the training is affecting the body size.

Another assessment method is to have a series of photographs taken of yourself in a swimsuit. Take photos of the front, side, and back, first with the body in a relaxed position and then with the muscles flexed. This information can be used later, after you have been training, to determine the changes that have taken place.

To a great extent, a person's body type is determined before birth, but through proper training, an individual can build some areas and reduce others. The purpose of this chapter is to explain various types of physique training programs one might engage in to bring about those body changes.

No one system of training is best because each individual is different. Experiment with different systems of training and find the method that works best. A combination of systems may bring about the desired results and stimulate the body to make rapid gains. Keep accurate records of how the body responds to the different methods of training. Comparing the progress made, makes it easier to select the most beneficial training regimen.

SYSTEMS OF TRAINING

Set System: The set system is the most popular type of training to develop strength. In this system the person does an exercise for a given number of repetitions, or a set, then rests before performing another set. A variation of this system is referred to as *supersets,* in which an exercise set for a particular muscle group is followed immediately by an exercise set for the antagonist muscle. For example, a person could do a set of arm curls for the biceps and then do a set of triceps extensions for the triceps. This combination would be one superset.

Another variation of this type of training is known as the super multiple set system. In this training system the lifter completes all of the sets for a given muscle group and then follows this exercise with the same number of sets for the antagonist muscle group.

Bodybuilding programs increase the volume of the workout by using more than one exercise for a given body part. They also utilize multiple sets and eight or more repetitions per set. As explained in chapter 3, increasing the volume provides the stimuli that is thought to bring about the metabolic changes that cause hypertrophy (an increase in muscle cell size).

Split Routine: In bodybuilding the idea is to exercise every major muscle group in the body. This requires a great amount of time and work. To obtain the maximum development, the major body parts are split into groups, and the lifter works out six days a week but exercises the selected body parts on alternate days. For example, the arms, legs, and midsection might be exercised on Monday, Wednesday, and Friday, and the chest, shoulders, and back would be exercised on Tuesday, Thursday, and Saturday. This system is one of the most popular types of training that bodybuilders use. Often this training program incorporates supersets.

A variation of the split-routine system is known as the *blitz method.* This method is often utilized when the bodybuilder is preparing for a contest and wishes to obtain the maximum size and muscle definition, which is so important in competition. In this system a person might perform all the arm exercises one day, all the chest exercises the next day, the legs on the next day, and so on. This is a very strenuous and tiring method of training and is usually recommended for only a few weeks at a time.

Burns: Some bodybuilders include sets of rapid half-contractions, or "burns," in their workout. These sets produce a burning sensation in the muscle, which is thought to be caused by blood being forced into the muscle area to produce the so-called *muscle pump.* The lifter is trying to achieve a greater increase in the size of the musculature.

Forced Reps: In the forced reps method of training, a partner assists the lifter so that more repetitions with greater resistance can be accomplished. The partner can push the individual far beyond the normal point of fatigue, the hoped-for result being more strength and muscle-building stimulation. For example, an individual might do ten repetitions on the lat pull-down without assistance. When the person reaches the normal point of fatigue on the tenth repetition, the partner would assist the lifter through the sticking point for three to five more forced reps.

Preexhaustion: Most exercises in strength training are accomplished by a large muscle group working in conjunction with a smaller muscle group. For example, the back muscles work with the biceps of the arm in pull-ups. The small muscle may fatigue before the large muscle group, and as a result, the large muscle group does not receive the optimum resistance to bring about physiological changes, such as an increase in size.

The preexhaustion system is based on the idea of doing a preliminary isolation exercise to overload the large muscle group before doing the exercise that uses both the large and small muscle groups together. This technique theoretically would then fatigue the stronger group to make it weaker than the smaller muscle group, thus enabling the lifter to push the basic combination exercise to a point where both muscle groups would develop.

Pyramid System: This type of training consists of adding weight until the lifter can complete only one repetition. For example, a person may start doing the bench press with a set of 10 RM, then add enough weight to do 9 RM, then 8 RM, and so on until the final set would consist of 1 RM.

In the first type of pyramid the lifter went from light to heavy resistance. In another pyramid system the lifter goes from heavy to light resistance. After a warm-up set the lifter does a set of 1 to 2 RM, removes, for example, five pounds, and does the maximum number of repetitions, continuing in this way until only the weight of the bar or a small resistance remains.

The following section is a training program utilized by a student who placed first in the Mr. Collegiate USA contest.

MR. COLLEGIATE USA TRAINING PROGRAM

BASIC CONCEPTS

1. Every major muscle group in the body is exercised.
2. The musculature is worked as thoroughly as possible (achieving a "pumped" feeling).
3. Every set is preceded by a rest period of no more than ninety seconds.
4. Every repetition is performed in the strictest form.
5. The emphasis in bodybuilding is placed on doing the exercise movement correctly rather than trying to lift as much weight as possible.
6. A set of high repetitions begins each initial exercise per major muscle group, and as the resistance increases, the repetitions decrease.

SPLIT-ROUTINE PROGRAM

Note: This program is to be followed six days a week. Exercise the midsection every day using a recovery time of two minutes.

First Day

Body Part	Exercise	
Midsection	Roman chair curl-up	3 sets of 75 reps, 3 sets of 80 reps
	V-sit	6 sets of 45 reps
	Hanging knee-up	6 sets of 25 reps
Biceps	Arm curl	1 set of 10 reps, 1 set of 8 reps, 3 sets of 6 reps
	Standing dumbbell curl	5 sets of 8 reps
	Incline dumbbell curl	5 sets of 8 reps
Triceps	Triceps press-down	4 sets of 8 reps, 1 set of 6 reps
	Lying barbell triceps extension	1 set of 20 reps, 4 sets of 8 reps
	Seated dumbbell triceps extension	2 sets of 10 reps, 2 sets of 8 reps, 1 set of 6 reps
Legs	Front squat	1 set of 20 reps, 1 set of 16 reps, 1 set of 12 reps, 1 set of 10 reps
	Lunge squat	1 set of 12 reps, 3 sets of 10 reps
	Leg curl	4 sets of 12 reps, 1 set of 20 reps
	Toe extension	5 sets of 20 reps, 3 sets of 25 reps
	Single-heel raise	6 sets of 8 reps

Second Day

Midsection	Roman chair curl-up	3 sets of 75 reps, 3 sets of 80 reps
	V-sit	6 sets of 45 reps
	Hanging knee-up	6 sets of 25 reps
Chest	Dumbbell bench press	1 set of 10 reps, 3 sets of 8 reps, 1 set of 6 reps
	Bench press to neck	1 set of 12 reps, 1 set of 10 reps, 2 sets of 8 reps, 1 set of 6 reps
	Decline press	1 set of 10 reps, 1 set of 8 reps, 2 sets of 6 reps
	Bench flys	2 sets of 10 reps, 1 set of 8 reps, 2 sets of 6 reps
Back	Close grip lat pull-down	2 sets of 10 reps, 2 sets of 9 reps
	Regular grip lat pull-down	1 set of 10 reps, 2 sets of 8 reps, 1 set of 7 reps
	Seated rowing	3 sets of 10 reps, 1 set of 9 reps
Shoulders	Seated behind-neck press	2 sets of 7 reps, 2 sets of 6 reps, 5 sets of 12 reps
	Seated dumbbell press	5 sets of 12 reps
	Upright rowing	1 set of 10 reps, 4 sets of 9 reps
	Side lateral raise	5 sets of 8 reps

THE SPORT EXPERIENCE

Write a bodybuilding training program for yourself using the bodybuilding worksheet in Appendix H. Keep the following guidelines in mind:

1. Before starting your bodybuilding program, take all of your body measurements using the body measurement chart in Appendix A so you can plot your progress as you train.
2. If possible, take some photographs of yourself before starting your training program to compare how you look at various stages of your training program.
3. Work every major muscle group in your body.
4. Experiment with various bodybuilding systems of training during your program to determine which works best for you.

APPENDIX A

Body Measurement Chart

Name _____ Age _____

	Date										
Body Weight											
Neck											
Shoulders											
Chest	Relaxed										
	Flexed										
Upper Arm											
Relaxed	Right										
	Left										
Flexed	Right										
	Left										
Forearm											
Relaxed	Right										
	Left										
Flexed	Right										
	Left										
Waist											
Hips											
Thigh											
Relaxed	Right										
	Left										
Flexed	Right										
	Left										
Calf											
Relaxed	Right										
	Left										
Flexed	Right										
	Left										
Other Body Parts											

APPENDIX A

Body Measurement Chart

Name _____ Age _____

	Date											
Body Weight												
Neck												
Shoulders												
Chest	Relaxed											
	Flexed											
Upper Arm												
Relaxed	Right											
	Left											
Flexed	Right											
	Left											
Forearm												
Relaxed	Right											
	Left											
Flexed	Right											
	Left											
Waist												
Hips												
Thigh												
Relaxed	Right											
	Left											
Flexed	Right											
	Left											
Calf												
Relaxed	Right											
	Left											
Flexed	Right											
	Left											
Other Body Parts												

APPENDIX A

Body Measurement Chart

Name _____ Age _____

Date												
Body Weight												
Neck												
Shoulders												
Chest — Relaxed												
Chest — Flexed												
Upper Arm												
Relaxed — Right												
Relaxed — Left												
Flexed — Right												
Flexed — Left												
Forearm												
Relaxed — Right												
Relaxed — Left												
Flexed — Right												
Flexed — Left												
Waist												
Hips												
Thigh												
Relaxed — Right												
Relaxed — Left												
Flexed — Right												
Flexed — Left												
Calf												
Relaxed — Right												
Relaxed — Left												
Flexed — Right												
Flexed — Left												
Other Body Parts												

APPENDIX A

Body Measurement Chart

Name _____ Age _____

Date											
Body Weight											
Neck											
Shoulders											
Chest — Relaxed											
Chest — Flexed											
Upper Arm											
Relaxed — Right											
Relaxed — Left											
Flexed — Right											
Flexed — Left											
Forearm											
Relaxed — Right											
Relaxed — Left											
Flexed — Right											
Flexed — Left											
Waist											
Hips											
Thigh											
Relaxed — Right											
Relaxed — Left											
Flexed — Right											
Flexed — Left											
Calf											
Relaxed — Right											
Relaxed — Left											
Flexed — Right											
Flexed — Left											
Other Body Parts											

APPENDIX
B

Strength Test

Name _____

PROCEDURES FOR ADMINISTERING STRENGTH TEST

1. Familiarize Yourself with the six exercises utilized for the test.
   a. Lat Pull-Down (LPD)—Start in a seated position and have someone hold the subject down at the shoulders. (page 111)
   b. Leg Extension (LE) (page 125)
   c. Bench Press (BP) (page 103)
   d. Curl-Up (CU)—Hold the weight on the front of the forehead, keep the knees flexed at a 100° angle, and have someone hold the feet. Curl forward and touch the elbows to the knees. (page 121)
   e. Leg Curl (LC)—flex the knee until the subject reaches a 90° angle. (page 148)
   f. Arm Curl (AC) (page 75)
2. Determine subject's weight in pounds.
3. Determine the amount of resistance to be used for each exercise. To obtain this number, multiply the body weight by the percentage of body weight given for each exercise in the chart at the bottom of the worksheet. Round the number to the lowest five pounds. For example, 54 is rounded to 50.
4. Record your resistance in the bottom of the worksheet.
5. Perform the maximum continuous number of repetitions for each exercise.
6. Determine the percentile rank for each exercise.

Strength Test

	Men							Women					
% Rank	LPD	LE	BP	CU	LC	AC	% Rank	LPD	LE	BP	CU	LC	AC
90	19	19	19	23	19	19	90	21	18	20	22	12	20
80	16	15	16	17	15	15	80	16	13	16	14	10	16
70	13	14	13	14	13	12	70	13	11	13	11	9	14
60	11	13	11	12	11	10	60	11	10	11	6	7	12
50	10	12	10	10	10	9	50	10	9	10	5	6	10
40	9	10	7	8	8	8	40	9	8	5	4	5	8
30	7	9	5	5	6	7	30	7	7	3	2	4	7
20	6	7	3	3	4	5	20	6	5	1	1	3	6
10	4	5	1	2	3	3	10	3	3	0	0	1	3
5	3	3	0	1	1	2	5	2	1	0	0	0	2

Adapted from the test developed by W. W. K. Hoeger and D. R. Hopkins and used with their permission.

7. Determine the strength category and number of points for each exercise.

% Rank	90	80–89	60–79	40–59	20–39	10–19	less than 10
Strength Category	Superior	Excellent	Good	Average	Fair	Poor	Very Poor
Points	19	17	15	13	11	9	7

8. Record percentile rank, strength category, and number of points below.

Exercise	% Body Weight		Resistance	Reps	% Rank	Strength Category	Pts
	Men	Women					
1. Lat Pull-Down	.70	.45					
2. Leg Extension	.65	.50					
3. Bench Press	.75	.45					
4. Curl-Up	.16	.10					
5. Leg Curl	.32	.25					
6. Arm Curl	.35	.18					

Total Points

APPENDIX
B
Strength Test

Name _____

PROCEDURES FOR ADMINISTERING STRENGTH TEST
1. Familiarize Yourself with the six exercises utilized for the test.
   a. Lat Pull-Down (LPD)—Start in a seated position and have someone hold the subject down at the shoulders. (page 111)
   b. Leg Extension (LE) (page 125)
   c. Bench Press (BP) (page 103)
   d. Curl-Up (CU)—Hold the weight on the front of the forehead, keep the knees flexed at a 100° angle, and have someone hold the feet. Curl forward and touch the elbows to the knees. (page 121)
   e. Leg Curl (LC)—flex the knee until the subject reaches a 90° angle. (page 148)
   f. Arm Curl (AC) (page 75)
2. Determine subject's weight in pounds.
3. Determine the amount of resistance to be used for each exercise. To obtain this number, multiply the body weight by the percentage of body weight given for each exercise in the chart at the bottom of the worksheet. Round the number to the lowest five pounds. For example, 54 is rounded to 50.
4. Record your resistance in the bottom of the worksheet.
5. Perform the maximum continuous number of repetitions for each exercise.
6. Determine the percentile rank for each exercise.

Strength Test

	Men						Women						
% Rank	LPD	LE	BP	CU	LC	AC	% Rank	LPD	LE	BP	CU	LC	AC
90	19	19	19	23	19	19	90	21	18	20	22	12	20
80	16	15	16	17	15	15	80	16	13	16	14	10	16
70	13	14	13	14	13	12	70	13	11	13	11	9	14
60	11	13	11	12	11	10	60	11	10	11	6	7	12
50	10	12	10	10	10	9	50	10	9	10	5	6	10
40	9	10	7	8	8	8	40	9	8	5	4	5	8
30	7	9	5	5	6	7	30	7	7	3	2	4	7
20	6	7	3	3	4	5	20	6	5	1	1	3	6
10	4	5	1	2	3	3	10	3	3	0	0	1	3
5	3	3	0	1	1	2	5	2	1	0	0	0	2

Adapted from the test developed by W. W. K. Hoeger and D. R. Hopkins and used with their permission.

7. Determine the strength category and number of points for each exercise.

% Rank	90	80–89	60–79	40–59	20–39	10–19	less than 10
Strength Category	Superior	Excellent	Good	Average	Fair	Poor	Very Poor
Points	19	17	15	13	11	9	7

8. Record percentile rank, strength category, and number of points below.

| Exercise | % Body Weight | | Resistance | Reps | % Rank | Strength Category | Pts |
	Men	Women					
1. Lat Pull-Down	.70	.45					
2. Leg Extension	.65	.50					
3. Bench Press	.75	.45					
4. Curl-Up	.16	.10					
5. Leg Curl	.32	.25					
6. Arm Curl	.35	.18					

Total Points

APPENDIX
B

Strength Test

Name _____

PROCEDURES FOR ADMINISTERING STRENGTH TEST

1. Familiarize Yourself with the six exercises utilized for the test.
   a. Lat Pull-Down (LPD)—Start in a seated position and have someone hold the subject down at the shoulders. (page 111)
   b. Leg Extension (LE) (page 115)
   c. Bench Press (BP) (page 103)
   d. Curl-Up (CU)—Hold the weight on the front of the forehead, keep the knees flexed at a 100° angle, and have someone hold the feet. Curl forward and touch the elbows to the knees. (page 121)
   e. Leg Curl (LC)—flex the knee until the subject reaches a 90° angle. (page 148)
   f. Arm Curl (AC) (page 75)
2. Determine subject's weight in pounds.
3. Determine the amount of resistance to be used for each exercise. To obtain this number, multiply the body weight by the percentage of body weight given for each exercise in the chart at the bottom of the worksheet. Round the number to the lowest five pounds. For example, 54 is rounded to 50.
4. Record your resistance in the bottom of the worksheet.
5. Perform the maximum continuous number of repetitions for each exercise.
6. Determine the percentile rank for each exercise.

Strength Test

	Men							Women					
% Rank	LPD	LE	BP	CU	LC	AC	% Rank	LPD	LE	BP	CU	LC	AC
90	19	19	19	23	19	19	90	21	18	20	22	12	20
80	16	15	16	17	15	15	80	16	13	16	14	10	16
70	13	14	13	14	13	12	70	13	11	13	11	9	14
60	11	13	11	12	11	10	60	11	10	11	6	7	12
50	10	12	10	10	10	9	50	10	9	10	5	6	10
40	9	10	7	8	8	8	40	9	8	5	4	5	8
30	7	9	5	5	6	7	30	7	7	3	2	4	7
20	6	7	3	3	4	5	20	6	5	1	1	3	6
10	4	5	1	2	3	3	10	3	3	0	0	1	3
5	3	3	0	1	1	2	5	2	1	0	0	0	2

Adapted from the test developed by W. W. K. Hoeger and D. R. Hopkins and used with their permission.

7. Determine the strength category and number of points for each exercise.

% Rank	90	80–89	60–79	40–59	20–39	10–19	less than 10
Strength Category	Superior	Excellent	Good	Average	Fair	Poor	Very Poor
Points	19	17	15	13	11	9	7

8. Record percentile rank, strength category, and number of points below.

Exercise	% Body Weight		Resistance	Reps	% Rank	Strength Category	Pts
	Men	Women					
1. Lat Pull-Down	.70	.45					
2. Leg Extension	.65	.50					
3. Bench Press	.75	.45					
4. Curl-Up	.16	.10					
5. Leg Curl	.32	.25					
6. Arm Curl	.35	.18					

Total Points

APPENDIX
B
Strength Test

Name _____

PROCEDURES FOR ADMINISTERING STRENGTH TEST

1. Familiarize Yourself with the six exercises utilized for the test.
   a. Lat Pull-Down (LPD)—Start in a seated position and have someone hold the subject down at the shoulders. (page 111)
   b. Leg Extension (LE) (page 125)
   c. Bench Press (BP) (page 103)
   d. Curl-Up (CU)—Hold the weight on the front of the forehead, keep the knees flexed at a 100° angle, and have someone hold the feet. Curl forward and touch the elbows to the knees. (page 121)
   e. Leg Curl (LC)—flex the knee until the subject reaches a 90° angle. (page 148)
   f. Arm Curl (AC) (page 75)
2. Determine subject's weight in pounds.
3. Determine the amount of resistance to be used for each exercise. To obtain this number, multiply the body weight by the percentage of body weight given for each exercise in the chart at the bottom of the worksheet. Round the number to the lowest five pounds. For example, 54 is rounded to 50.
4. Record your resistance in the bottom of the worksheet.
5. Perform the maximum continuous number of repetitions for each exercise.
6. Determine the percentile rank for each exercise.

Strength Test

	Men							Women					
% Rank	LPD	LE	BP	CU	LC	AC	% Rank	LPD	LE	BP	CU	LC	AC
90	19	19	19	23	19	19	90	21	18	20	22	12	20
80	16	15	16	17	15	15	80	16	13	16	14	10	16
70	13	14	13	14	13	12	70	13	11	13	11	9	14
60	11	13	11	12	11	10	60	11	10	11	6	7	12
50	10	12	10	10	10	9	50	10	9	10	5	6	10
40	9	10	7	8	8	8	40	9	8	5	4	5	8
30	7	9	5	5	6	7	30	7	7	3	2	4	7
20	6	7	3	3	4	5	20	6	5	1	1	3	6
10	4	5	1	2	3	3	10	3	3	0	0	1	3
5	3	3	0	1	1	2	5	2	1	0	0	0	2

Adapted from the test developed by W. W. K. Hoeger and D. R. Hopkins and used with their permission.

7. Determine the strength category and number of points for each exercise.

% Rank	90	80–89	60–79	40–59	20–39	10–19	less than 10
Strength Category	Superior	Excellent	Good	Average	Fair	Poor	Very Poor
Points	19	17	15	13	11	9	7

8. Record percentile rank, strength category, and number of points below.

Exercise	% Body Weight		Resistance	Reps	% Rank	Strength Category	Pts
	Men	Women					
1. Lat Pull-Down	.70	.45					
2. Leg Extension	.65	.50					
3. Bench Press	.75	.45					
4. Curl-Up	.16	.10					
5. Leg Curl	.32	.25					
6. Arm Curl	.35	.18					

Total Points

APPENDIX
C

Strength Training Record

Name _____ Age _____

Date					
Exercise	Wt Reps	Wt Reps	Wt Reps	Wt Reps	Wt Reps

APPENDIX C

Strength Training Record

Name _____ Age _____

Date / Exercise	Wt Reps	Wt Reps	Wt Reps	Wt Reps	Wt Reps

APPENDIX C

Strength Training Record

Name _____ Age _____

Date Exercise	Wt Reps	Wt Reps	Wt Reps	Wt Reps	Wt Reps

APPENDIX
C

Strength Training Record

Name _____ Age _____

Date					
Exercise	Wt Reps	Wt Reps	Wt Reps	Wt Reps	Wt Reps

APPENDIX D

Strength Training Worksheet

Name _____   Recovery _____

Body Part	Exercise	Sets	Reps	Resistance
Chest				
Midsection				
Triceps				
Legs				
Shoulders				
Neck				
Biceps				
Back				
Wrists				

APPENDIX D

Strength Training Worksheet

Name _____   Recovery _____

Body Part	Exercise	Sets	Reps	Resistance
Chest				
Midsection				
Triceps				
Legs				
Shoulders				
Neck				
Biceps				
Back				
Wrists				

APPENDIX
D

Strength Training Worksheet

Name _____ Recovery _____

Body Part	Exercise	Sets	Reps	Resistance
Chest				
Midsection				
Triceps				
Legs				
Shoulders				
Neck				
Biceps				
Back				
Wrists				

APPENDIX
D
Strength Training Worksheet

Name _____   Recovery _____

Body Part	Exercise	Sets	Reps	Resistance
Chest				
Midsection				
Triceps				
Legs				
Shoulders				
Neck				
Biceps				
Back				
Wrists				

Sports Training Worksheet

Name _____ Sport _____ Position _____
Period _____
Core Exercises: Recovery _____
Supplementary Exercises:

Body Part	Exercise	Sets	Reps	Resistance
Chest				
Midsection				
Triceps				
Legs				
Shoulders				
Neck				
Biceps				
Back				
Wrists				

APPENDIX E

Sports Training Worksheet

Name _____ Sport _____ Position _____

Period _____

Core Exercises: Recovery _____

Supplementary Exercises:

Body Part	Exercise	Sets	Reps	Resistance
Chest				
Midsection				
Triceps				
Legs				
Shoulders				
Neck				
Biceps				
Back				
Wrists				

APPENDIX E

Sports Training Worksheet

Name _____ Sport _____ Position _____
Period _____
Core Exercises: Recovery _____
Supplementary Exercises:

Body Part	Exercise	Sets	Reps	Resistance
Chest				
Midsection				
Triceps				
Legs				
Shoulders				
Neck				
Biceps				
Back				
Wrists				

APPENDIX E

Sports Training Worksheet

Name _____ Sport _____ Position _____

Period _____

Core Exercises: Recovery _____

Supplementary Exercises:

Body Part	Exercise	Sets	Reps	Resistance
Chest				
Midsection				
Triceps				
Legs				
Shoulders				
Neck				
Biceps				
Back				
Wrists				

Modified Periodization Worksheet

Name _____

Sports _____

Positions _____

In-Season ☐   Off-Season ☐

Core Exercises

Five-set Day: 3 sets × 4 reps at 80% 1 RM
                2 sets × 2 reps at 90% 1 RM
Three-set Day: 2 sets × 4 reps at 80% 1 RM
                1 set × 2 reps at 90% 1 RM

Recovery Time: _____

Exercise	1 RM	80% 1 RM	90% 1 RM

Supplementary Exercises

Exercise	Sets	Reps	Recovery	Resistance

Modified Periodization Worksheet

Name _____

Sports _____

Positions _____

In-Season ☐   Off-Season ☐

Core Exercises

Five-set Day:	3 sets × 4 reps at 80% 1 RM
	2 sets × 2 reps at 90% 1 RM
Three-set Day:	2 sets × 4 reps at 80% 1 RM
	1 set × 2 reps at 90% 1 RM

Recovery Time: _____

Exercise	1 RM	80% 1 RM	90% 1 RM

Supplementary Exercises

Exercise	Sets	Reps	Recovery	Resistance

APPENDIX
F

Modified Periodization Worksheet

Name _____

Sports _____

Positions _____

In-Season ☐   Off-Season ☐

Core Exercises

Five-set Day: 3 sets × 4 reps at 80% 1 RM
                2 sets × 2 reps at 90% 1 RM
Three-set Day: 2 sets × 4 reps at 80% 1 RM
                1 set × 2 reps at 90% 1 RM

Recovery Time: _____

Exercise	1 RM	80% 1 RM	90% 1 RM

Supplementary Exercises

Exercise	Sets	Reps	Recovery	Resistance

APPENDIX F

Modified Periodization Worksheet

Name _____

Sports _____

Positions _____

In-Season ☐   Off-Season ☐

Core Exercises

Five-set Day: 3 sets × 4 reps at 80% 1 RM
                 2 sets × 2 reps at 90% 1 RM
Three-set Day: 2 sets × 4 reps at 80% 1 RM
                 1 set × 2 reps at 90% 1 RM

Recovery Time: _____

Exercise	1 RM	80% 1 RM	90% 1 RM

Supplementary Exercises

Exercise	Sets	Reps	Recovery	Resistance

APPENDIX
G
Nebraska Athletic Test

Name _____

Ten-yard dash	Time: _____
Forty-yard dash	Time: _____
Twenty-yard shuttle run	Time: _____
Vertical Jump	Height: _____

SHUTTLE RUN

Procedure: Draw two lines parallel to and five yards on either side of a center line. Begin the test in a three-point stance straddling the center line. The person timing starts the stopwatch with the first movement. The athlete then turns and runs either right or left to an outer line; touches the surface beyond the line; then reverses direction and runs and touches the surface beyond the other outside line; reverses direction again and finishes by crossing the center line.

VERTICAL JUMP

Procedure: Stand facing the measuring board with the dominant arm fully extended and hold a piece of chalk in the hand to mark the height. The athlete then goes to a squat position with the feet flat on the floor. The athlete then jumps as high as possible and touches the measuring board with the chalk at the height of the jump. The vertical jump score is the difference between the first and second chalk marks.

APPENDIX
G

Nebraska Athletic Test

Name _____

Ten-yard dash   Time: _____
Forty-yard dash   Time: _____
Twenty-yard shuttle run   Time: _____
Vertical Jump   Height: _____

SHUTTLE RUN

Procedure: Draw two lines parallel to and five yards on either side of a center line. Begin the test in a three-point stance straddling the center line. The person timing starts the stopwatch with the first movement. The athlete then turns and runs either right or left to an outer line; touches the surface beyond the line; then reverses direction and runs and touches the surface beyond the other outside line; reverses direction again and finishes by crossing the center line.

VERTICAL JUMP

Procedure: Stand facing the measuring board with the dominant arm fully extended and hold a piece of chalk in the hand to mark the height. The athlete then goes to a squat position with the feet flat on the floor. The athlete then jumps as high as possible and touches the measuring board with the chalk at the height of the jump. The vertical jump score is the difference between the first and second chalk marks.

APPENDIX
G
Nebraska Athletic Test

Name _____

Ten-yard dash	Time: _____
Forty-yard dash	Time: _____
Twenty-yard shuttle run	Time: _____
Vertical Jump	Height: _____

SHUTTLE RUN

Procedure: Draw two lines parallel to and five yards on either side of a center line. Begin the test in a three-point stance straddling the center line. The person timing starts the stopwatch with the first movement. The athlete then turns and runs either right or left to an outer line; touches the surface beyond the line; then reverses direction and runs and touches the surface beyond the other outside line; reverses direction again and finishes by crossing the center line.

VERTICAL JUMP

Procedure: Stand facing the measuring board with the dominant arm fully extended and hold a piece of chalk in the hand to mark the height. The athlete then goes to a squat position with the feet flat on the floor. The athlete then jumps as high as possible and touches the measuring board with the chalk at the height of the jump. The vertical jump score is the difference between the first and second chalk marks.

APPENDIX
G

Nebraska Athletic Test

Name _____

Ten-yard dash	Time: _____
Forty-yard dash	Time: _____
Twenty-yard shuttle run	Time: _____
Vertical Jump	Height: _____

SHUTTLE RUN

Procedure: Draw two lines parallel to and five yards on either side of a center line. Begin the test in a three-point stance straddling the center line. The person timing starts the stopwatch with the first movement. The athlete then turns and runs either right or left to an outer line; touches the surface beyond the line; then reverses direction and runs and touches the surface beyond the other outside line; reverses direction again and finishes by crossing the center line.

VERTICAL JUMP

Procedure: Stand facing the measuring board with the dominant arm fully extended and hold a piece of chalk in the hand to mark the height. The athlete then goes to a squat position with the feet flat on the floor. The athlete then jumps as high as possible and touches the measuring board with the chalk at the height of the jump. The vertical jump score is the difference between the first and second chalk marks.

APPENDIX H

Bodybuilding Training Worksheet

Name _____   Recovery _____

Body Part	Exercise	Sets	Reps	Resistance
Chest				
Midsection				
Triceps				
Legs				
Shoulders				
Neck				
Biceps				
Back				
Wrists				

Bodybuilding Training Worksheet

Name _____   Recovery _____

Body Part	Exercise	Sets	Reps	Resistance
Chest				
Midsection				
Triceps				
Legs				
Shoulders				
Neck				
Biceps				
Back				
Wrists				

APPENDIX H

Bodybuilding Training Worksheet

Name _____ Recovery _____

Body Part	Exercise	Sets	Reps	Resistance
Chest				
Midsection				
Triceps				
Legs				
Shoulders				
Neck				
Biceps				
Back				
Wrists				

APPENDIX H

Bodybuilding Training Worksheet

Name _____   Recovery _____

Body Part	Exercise	Sets	Reps	Resistance
Chest				
Midsection				
Triceps				
Legs				
Shoulders				
Neck				
Biceps				
Back				
Wrists				

APPENDIX I

Periodicals on Strength Training

American Health and Fitness
Canusa Products, Inc.
2025 McKinley Street
Hollywood, FL 33020

Bigger, Faster, Stronger
BFS Publishing, Inc.
805 West 2400 South
Salt Lake City, UT 84119

Exercise and Health
Harris Publications, Inc.
1115 Broadway
New York, NY 10010

Flex
Weider Publications, Inc.
2100 Erwin Street
Woodland Hills, CA 91367

Ironman
Ironman Press
1701 Ives Avenue
Oxnard, CA 93033

Journal of Strength and
  Conditioning Research
National Strength and
  Conditioning Association
1955 North Union Boulevard
Colorado Springs, CO 80905

Men's Fitness
Weider Publications, Inc.
2100 Erwin Street
Woodland Hills, CA 91367

Muscle and Fitness
Weider Publications, Inc.
2100 Erwin Street
Woodland Hills, CA 91367

Muscle Media
Muscle Media Publishing, Inc.
555 Corporate Circle
Golden, CO 80401

Strength and Conditioning Journal
National Strength and
  Conditioning Association
1955 North Union Boulevard
Colorado Springs, CO 80905

Training and Conditioning
MAG, Inc.
2488 North Triphammer Road
Ithaca, NY 14850

Women's Physique World
Women's Physique World, Inc.
P.O. Box 429
Midland Park, NJ 07432

BIBLIOGRAPHY

Allsen, Philip E., Joyce M. Harrison, and Barbara Vance. *Fitness for Life: An Individualized Approach.* 6th ed. Madison Wis.: McGraw Hill, 1997.

American College of Sports Medicine. "Position Stand on Progression Models in Resistance Training for Healthy Adults." *Medicine and Science in Sports* 34, no. 2 (2002): 364–80.

————. "Position Statement on the Use and Abuse of Anabolic-Androgenic Steroids in Sport." *Medicine and Science in Sports* 19, no. 5 (1987): 534–39.

Baechle, Thomas R., and Roger W. Earle, eds. *Essentials of Strength Training and Conditioning.* 2^d ed. Champaign, Ill.: Human Kinetics, 2000.

Bompa, Tudor O. *Periodization of Strength.* Toronto, Ontario, Canada: Veritas, 1993.

Delavier, Frederic. *Strength Training Anatomy.* Champaign, Ill.: Human Kinetics, 2001.

Hatfield, Frederick C., and March L. Krotee. *Personalized Weight Training for Fitness and Athletics: From Theory to Practice.* 2^d ed. Dubuque, Iowa: Kendall/Hunt, 1994.

Hesson, James L. *Weight Training for Life.* 5th ed. Englewood, Colo.: Morton, 2000.

McComas, Alan J. *Skeletal Muscle: Form and Function.* Champaign, Ill.: Human Kinetics, 1996.

Shepard, Greg. *Bigger, Faster, Stronger.* Salt Lake City, Utah: BFS, 1996.

Sienna, Phillip A. *One Rep Max: A Guide to Beginning Weight Training.* Madison, Wis.: Brown and Benchmark, 1989.

Wescott, Wayne. *Be Strong: Strength Training for Muscular Fitness for Men and Women.* Madison, Wis.: Brown and Benchmark, 1993.

Williams, Melvin H. *Nutrition for Fitness and Sport.* 4th ed. Madison, Wis.:Brown and Benchmark, 1995.

INDEX

Isokinetic training, 28
Isolation exercise, 168
Isometric action, 28
Isometric strength programs, 29–30

J
Joint-lever systems
  principles of, 12–17
  weakest joint angle principle and, 17–18
Journal of Strength and Conditioning Research, 235

K
Keys, Ancel, 3
Krotee, March L., 53

L
Lat Pull-Down (LPD)
  for backs, 112
  for specific sports, 158, 161
  split-routine program and, 170
  Strength Test (appendix) and, 179–186
Latissimus dorsi, 24
Law of specificity, 28
Lean body mass, 3
Leg Curl (LC)
  method, 148
  for specific sports, 158, 161
  split-routine program and, 169
  Strength Test (appendix) and, 179–186
Leg Extension (LE), 136, 158, 161, 179–186
Leg Press (LP), 135, 157–158, 161
Leg Splits, 129
Legs
  Bench Jump, 138
  Bodybuilding Training Worksheet (appendix) and, 227–234
  Donkey Raise, 144
  Dumbbell Jump Squat, 137
  exercises for, 69
  Front Leg Kick, 145
  Front Squat, 131
  Glute-Ham Raise, 149
  Hack Squat, 132
  Leg Curl (LC), 148, 158, 161, 169, 179–186
  Leg Extension (LE), 136, 158, 161, 179–186
  Leg Press (LP), 135, 157–158, 161

Leg Splits, 129
Lunge Squat, 133, 169
Power Clean, 150–151, 157–158, 161
Side Leg Kick, 146
Single-Heel Raise, 140
Sitting Heel Raise, 141
split routine program and, 169–170
Sports Training Worksheet (appendix) and, 203–210
Squats, 130, 157–158, 161
Standing Heel Raise, 139
Strength Training Worksheet (appendix) and, 195–202
Toe Extension, 142
Toe Raise, 143
Trap Bar, 134
Vertical Leg Press, 147
Levator scapulae, 23
Liver, dessicated, as dietary supplements, 40–41
Lunge Squat, 133, 169
Lying Barbell Triceps Extension, 88, 169
Lying Dumbbell Triceps Extension, 90

M
Ma huang, as dietary supplements, 42–43
Machines. *See* Equipment
Major rhomboids, 23
Maximum resistance, 28
Measurements. *See* Body measurements
Mechanical advantage, 17
Medium chain triglycerides (MTC), as dietary supplements, 42–43
Men's Fitness, 235
Midsection
  Bodybuilding Training Worksheet (appendix) and, 227–234
  Curl-Up, 121–122
  exercises for, 69
  Hanging Knee-Up, 125
  Roman Chair Curl-Up, 124
  Side Bend, 127
  Sitting Knee-Up, 126
  split routine program and, 169–170
  Sports Training Worksheet (appendix) and, 203–210
  Strength Training Worksheet (appendix) and, 195–202
  Twists, 128
  V-Sit, 123

Minimum resistance, 47
Minor rhomboid, 23
Modified periodization program, 163
Modified Periodization Worksheet
(appendix), 211–218
Mormon tea. *See* Ma huang
Motor unit test, 12
Motor units
atrophy and, 17
principles of, 9–12
Mr. Collegiate USA Training
Program, 168
Muscle action, 21
Muscle and Fitness, 235
Muscle cell, 16
Muscle Media, 235
Muscle pump, 167
Muscles. *see also specific muscle, i.e.*
Flexor pollicis longus
actions/sports use of, 18–27
delayed onset muscle soreness (DOMS)
and, 56–57
joint-lever systems and, 15–17
motor units and, 9
Muscle-boundness, 4
Muscular endurance, 29
Muscularity, 165
Myofibrils, 17

N
National Strength and Conditioning
Association, 6
Nebraska Athletic Test, 164, 219–226
Neck
Bodybuilding Training Worksheet
(appendix) and, 227–234
exercises for specific sports, 158, 161
Sports Training Worksheet (appendix)
and, 203–210
Strength Training Worksheet
(appendix) and, 195–202
Neck Strap, 72
Nervous tissue and joint-lever systems,
13–14
Nutrition
anabolic steroids and, 34–35
benefits/efficacy/safety of dietary
supplements, 36–45
strength development and, 31–33

O
Off-season training program, 162–163
Older people and strength training, 5
One set only, 49
Osteoporosis, 14–15
Overhead press, 158, 161
Overload principle, 27–28, 71
Overtraining, 154–155

P
Pangamic acid, as dietary supplements,
42–43
Partner Resistance, 73
Pectoralis major, 23
Periodicals on Strength Training, 235
Periodization
definition, 20
Modified Periodization Worksheet
(appendix), 211–218
for off-season program, 163
peak performance and, 154–157
recommendation of, 52
Periodization phases, 156
Peroneus brevis, 26
Peroneus longus, 26
Personalized Weight Training for
Fitness and Athletics: From Theory
to Practice, 53
Phosphagen, 51
Phosphate salts, as dietary supplements,
44–45
Phosphocreatine, 50
Photographs as assessment methods, 166
Physiological changes, 13
Physique, 29
Physique athletes, 165
Plantaris, 26
Popliteus, 26
Power, 1
Power Clean
as core exercise, 157
method, 150–151
for specific sports, 158, 161
Preacher-board Curl, 77
Preexhaustion, 167–168
Presentation, 165
Progressive resistance training, 29
Pronator quadratus, 22
Pronator teres, 22

V

V-Sit, 123, 169–170
Valsalva effect, 54
Variable resistance, 29–31
Vastus lateralis, 26
Vastus medialis, 26
Velocity, 2
Vertical jump, 219–226
Vertical Leg Press, 147
Volume, 49, 155

W

Warm-up exercises
  delayed onset muscle soreness (DOMS)
    and, 56–57
  safety and, 55
  strength training for children and, 6
Weakest joint-angle principle, 17
Weight. *See* Body weight; Free weights
Weight lifting
  belts for, 55–56
  definition, 29
Weight training, 29

Williams, Melvin, 33
Women and strength training, 5
Women's Physique World, 235
Wrestler's Bridge, 74
Wrist Curl, 94, 158, 161
Wrist Roller, 98
Wrists
  Bodybuilding Training Worksheet
    (appendix) and, 227–234
  Dumbbell Wrist Curl, 96
  exercises for, 68
  Reverse Dumbbell Wrist Curl, 97
  Reverse Wrist Curl, 95
  Sports Training Worksheet (appendix)
    and, 203–210
  Strength Training Worksheet
    (appendix) and, 195–202
  Wrist Curl, 94, 158, 161
  Wrist Roller, 98

Y

Yohimbe (yohimbine), as dietary
  supplements, 44–45